THE LIVING BREAD

BOOKS BY THOMAS MERTON

The Asian Journal
Bread in the Wilderness
Conjectures of a Guilty Bystander
Contemplation in a World of Action
Disputed Questions
Gandhi on Non-Violence
Ishi Means Man
Life and Holiness
The Living Bread
Love and Living
The Monastic Journey
My Argument with the Gestapo
Mystics and Zen Masters
The New Man
New Seeds of Contemplation
No Man Is an Island
Seasons of Celebration
The Secular Journal of Thomas Merton
Seeds of Destruction
The Seven Storey Mountain
The Sign of Jonas
The Silent Life
Thoughts in Solitude
The Waters of Siloe
Zen and the Birds of Appetite

POETRY

The Collected Poems of Thomas Merton
Emblems of a Season of Fury
The Strange Islands
Selected Poems
The Tears of the Blind Lions

TRANSLATIONS

Clement of Alexandria
The Way of Chuang Tzu
The Wisdom of the Desert

THE
LIVING
BREAD

BY THOMAS MERTON

"I am the living bread that has come
down from heaven. If anyone eat
of this bread, he shall live forever."
JOHN 6: 51–52

Farrar • Straus • Giroux / New York

Published in Canada by
McGraw-Hill Ryerson Ltd., Toronto

Library of Congress Cataloging in Publication Data
Merton, Thomas, 1915-1968.
The Living Bread.
Includes bibliographical references.
1. Lord's Supper—Catholic Church.   I. Title.
BX2215.2.M44 1980   264'.0203   79-6352

Cum permissu superiorum

CONTENTS

V O SACREM CONVIVIUM

PROLOGUE

Christianity is more than a doctrine. It is Christ Himself, living in those whom He has united to Himself in one Mystical Body. It is the mystery by which the Incarnation of the Word of God continues and extends itself throughout the history of the world, reaching into the souls and lives of all men, until the final completion of God's plan. Christianity is the "re-establishment of all things in Christ" (Ephesians 1:10).

Now Christ lives and acts in men by faith and by the sacraments of faith. The greatest of all the sacraments, the crown of the whole Christian life on earth, is the Sacrament of charity, the Blessed Eucharist, in which Christ not only gives us grace but actually gives us Himself. For in this most Holy Sacrament Jesus Christ Himself is truly and substantially present, and remains present as long as the consecrated species of bread and wine continue in existence. The Blessed Eucharist is therefore the very heart of Christianity since it contains Christ Himself, and since it is the chief means by which

Christ mystically unites the faithful to Himself in one Body.

Furthermore, since the Passion of Christ is the center of human history, and since the eucharistic sacrifice makes present on the altar the Sacrifice of Calvary, by which man is redeemed, the Eucharist re-enacts the most important event in the history of mankind. It communicates to all men the fruits of Redemption. Yet there is something else. The Blessed Eucharist not only perpetuates the Incarnation of the Son of God and keeps Him present among us even bodily, it not only makes present the death by which He sacrificed Himself, for love of us, on the Cross, but it even reaches forward into the future and represents the consummation of all man's history: the Eucharist is a prophetic sign of the Last Judgment and of the general resurrection and of our entrance into glory.[1]

The Blessed Sacrament is then a memorial of all God's wonderful works, their epitome, the one Mystery which contains all other mysteries in itself. It is the central mystery of Christianity. "It is by this Sacrament that the Church continues in existence, by this Sacrament that faith is made strong, that the Christian religion and divine wor-

---

[1] In the Ambrosian Liturgy, we read: "Haec quotiescumque feceritis in mei commemorationis facieties, mortem meam praedicabitis, resurrectionem meam annuntiabitis, adventum meum sperabitis, donec iterum de caelis veniam ad vos."

ship flourish. It is by reason of this Sacrament that Christ says: 'Behold I am with you all days even to the end of time' " (Matthew 28:20).[2]

Christ in this admirable mystery remains in the midst of us as "one we know not." He "comes unto His own," and sometimes it is all too true to say that even "His own do not receive Him." But if we study what our faith teaches us about the Blessed Eucharist, we will appreciate more and more the truth that this is indeed the Living Bread, the "Bread of God which comes down from heaven and gives life to the world" (John 6:33).

Christianity is a religion of life, not of death. It is the religion of the transcendent, Living God, Who is so far exalted above all our concepts of Him that we can only grasp Him remotely and indirectly, by analogy, and Who is yet so close to us that our most intimate knowledge of Him is closely related to the secret knowledge we possess of our own deepest self.

The Living God, transcendent and immanent, the Alpha and the Omega, the beginning and the end, the One Who is everywhere and nowhere, makes Himself visible and tangible and gives Himself to us to be our spiritual food in the Blessed Eucharist.

The Blessed Eucharist is therefore not merely an

---

[2] St. Bonaventure, *De praeparatione ad Missam*, i, 3.

object of study and speculation. It is our very life. And indeed, because it is our life, if the Eucharist were to remain merely an object of study we would never really penetrate its ineffable mystery. For the mystery of life can only be known by being lived. And the Mystery of the Eucharist, the source of all our life in God, the source of all charity, can only be penetrated by being lived and loved. Christ in the Blessed Eucharist begins to reveal Himself to those who adore Him with humble faith and who receive Him into pure hearts with a true and sincere charity. He reveals Himself still more to those who leave everything else for love of Him. But He reveals Himself fully only to those who enter into the very mystery of His Passion and Death and Resurrection by loving their brethren with His own love, which is the wellspring of the whole mystery. In order to see something of the meaning of the Blessed Eucharist, we must see God and adore Him in this Sacrament. We must see in it the Passion of Christ. But above all we must *live* the Mystery of the Eucharist by offering ourselves to the Father with Jesus, and by loving others as Christ has loved us.

The whole problem of our time is the problem of love: how are we going to recover the ability to love ourselves and to love one another? The reason why we hate one another and fear one another is that we secretly or openly hate and fear

our own selves. And we hate ourselves because the
depths of our being are a chaos of frustration and
spiritual misery. Lonely and helpless, we cannot be
at peace with others because we are not at peace
with ourselves, and we cannot be at peace with
ourselves because we are not at peace with God.

Modern materialism has reached the point where
all its techniques tend to converge, systematically
or otherwise, upon the disintegration of man in
himself and in society. Totalitarian states ruthlessly
manipulate human beings, degrading and destroying
them at will, sacrificing bodies and minds on the
altar of political opportunism without the slightest
respect for the value of the human person. Indeed,
one might almost say that the modern dictatorships
have displayed everywhere a deliberate and calcu-
lated hatred for human nature as such. The techniques of degradation used in concentration camps
and in staged trials are too familiar to be detailed
here. They all have one purpose: to defile the
human person beyond recognition in order to man-
ufacture evidence for a lie.

Charity and trust which unite us to other men
by that very fact make us grow and develop within
ourselves. It is by well-ordered contact, by related-
ness with others, that we ourselves become mature
and responsible persons. Techniques of degradation
systematically foment distrust, resentment, separa-

tion and hatred. They keep men spiritually isolated from one another, while jamming them together physically on a superficial level—the plane of the mass meeting. They tend to corrode all man's personal relationships by fear and suspicion so that the neighbor, the co-worker, is not a friend and support but always a rival, a menace, a persecutor, a potential stool pigeon who, if we are not careful, will have us sent to prison.

Even where totalitarianism has not yet completely wiped out all liberty, men are still subject to the corrupting effect of materialism. The world has always been selfish: but the modern world has lost all ability to control its egoism. And yet, having acquired the power to satisfy its material needs and its desires for pleasures and comfort, it has discovered that these satisfactions are not enough. They do not bring peace, they do not bring happiness. They do not bring security either to the individual or to society. We live at the precise moment when the exorbitant optimism of the materialist world has plunged into spiritual ruin. We find ourselves living in a society of men who have discovered their own nonentity where they least expected to—in the midst of power and technological achievement. The result is an agony of ambivalence in which each man is forced to project upon his neighbors a burden of self-hatred which is too great to be tolerated by his own soul.

Constantly subject to the inexorable processes of spiritual erosion which gradually destroy our minds and wills, we know in the intimate depths of our being that our life must recover some unity, stability and meaning. We sense instinctively that these can only come to us from union with God and with one another. But under the steady bombardment of meaningless propaganda that is always directed against us, we surrender our privilege to think and hope and make decisions for ourselves. Passive and despairing, we allow ourselves to sink back into the inert mass of human objects that only exist to be manipulated by dictators, or by the great anonymous powers that rule the world of business. And we will never find God if we are not ourselves mature persons. To find God one must first be free.

When the Risen Christ founded His Church and commanded His Apostles to preach to all nations, He was offering mankind its only hope of true peace. The Church is the continuation of Christ's Incarnate life on earth, and Christ Himself is our peace (Ephesians 2:14). The Church, too, is the only institution in the world that can protect true liberty. She is in possession of the Truth which alone can make us free (John 8:32) for she is the Living Body of Christ; and Christ said "I am the Truth" (John 14:6). All who embrace the faith and truly enter into the Church's sacramental life will be free with that "freedom with which Christ has made us free" (Galatians 4:31), and indeed no Christian can allow himself in conscience to renounce that spiritual freedom which is his most precious inheritance. He cannot permit himself or his brothers in Christ to lose his appetite for life and joy in the possession of truth. No Christian can abandon himself passively to the ruthless forces that are destroying the unity and spirit of all mankind.

If therefore we would find peace, hope, certitude, spiritual security, we must seek Christ. But how? By mere outward enrollment in the Church as an organization, by mere conformity to certain rites, customs and practices? By subscribing to certain deeply formulated religious beliefs? No. These things are not enough. The Church is not only a social organization, but also and principally a Living Mystical Body. The Church is Christ. To be Christians, we must live by Christ. To conquer the forces of death and despair, we must unite ourselves mystically to Christ Who has overcome death and Who brings us life and hope. To overcome the world we must be united with Him by faith, for faith is the victory which overcomes the world (I John 5:4). We must all unite ourselves to Him in that supreme sacrifice of Himself in which He brought us peace with God and with one another. We must mystically die with Him on the Cross by that same death in which "He reconciled all in one body to God, having slain all enmities in Himself"

(Ephesians 2:16). In a word, to find Christ we must not only believe and be baptized in the Name of the Father, the Son and the Holy Ghost, thus becoming His members: we must go on to crown our sacramental life in Christ by partaking of the Living Bread of the Eucharist, the supersubstantial Bread which imparts, to those who receive it, everlasting life.

Life in Christ! Christ living in us! Incorporation in Christ! Unity in Christ! These expressions tell us something of the meaning of the greatest of all sacraments, the Blessed Eucharist, the Sacrament of charity, the Sacrament of peace.

The Eucharist is the Sacrament of the Body and Blood of Jesus Christ. In promising us this Sacrament, Jesus described it in terms which are clear and simple, though they contain a tremendous mystery: "The bread which I shall give is my flesh, for the life of the world" (John 6:52). We who eat His Body and drink His Blood receive life in Him and from Him. But living by this miraculous Bread, we also find that we are united to one another. For, as St. Paul says, "Because the bread is one, we though many, are one body, all of us who partake of the one bread" (I Corinthians 10:17). In eating the sacramental Body of Christ we are absorbed into the Mystical Body of Christ. In Holy Communion, as we take Him to ourselves in the great sacrificial mystery which is the supreme expression of divine charity, we find that His charity gains possession of our souls and unites us to one another with a love so pure, so spiritual and so intense that it transcends all the powers of man's natural love for his brother and for his friend. The charity of Christ in the Eucharist, seizing upon the best natural instincts of the human soul, elevates and divinizes them, uniting men to one another in a charity and a peace which this world can never give.

A modern theologian writes:

Christ the Redeemer, who assimilates Christians to Himself, is Christ in His greatest act of love.... This love permeates Christians and transforms them into Himself: Therefore the Eucharist is the sacrament of charity. We honor it more by devotedness to our fellow men than by an ornate ceremonial, though the latter is also indispensable. The love it engenders for God and our neighbor, by assimilating us to Christ's integral love and incorporating us into Him, is in turn integral love, the love that cannot stop short at the complete gift of self.[3]

Active participation in the Mass, intelligent and humble reception of the Blessed Sacrament with a pure heart and the desire of perfect charity—these are the great remedies for the resentment and dis-

[3] E. Mersch, *The Theology of The Mystical Body*, p. 592.

unity that are spread by materialism. Here in this greatest of sacraments we can find the medicine that will purify our hearts from the contagion which they inevitably contract in a world that does not know God.

But in order to protect ourselves still more, to strengthen our position and to sink our roots deeper into the charity of Christ, it is necessary that we seek opportunities to adore Christ in this Blessed Sacrament and to give testimony to our faith outside the time of Mass. Therefore we visit our churches in order to pray to Him in silence and alone. We go to benediction of the Blessed Sacrament. We make Holy Hours, or we spend time in adoration, by day or by night, before the Sacramental Christ enthroned upon the altar. All these contacts deepen our awareness of the great mystery that is the very heart of the Church and open our souls to the influence of the Son of God "Who gives life to whom He wills" (John 5:21).

The Spirit of God, working in the Church and filling her members ever more abundantly with the light and strength of Christ in proportion as they have been attacked and persecuted by the enemies of truth, has inspired men to react against the evils of our time by a revival of all the aspects of the Catholic life of prayer.

First of all, the Holy Spirit has been teaching us, principally through the Holy Father in His Encyclicals, that the Christian life of prayer is and must remain an organic unity, of which the very heart is the Mystery of the Eucharist. The divine grace which diffuses itself from this center throughout the whole body of our prayer-life travels through the arteries which are provided by the various forms of liturgical worship—sacraments and sacramentals. In order for this bloodstream of grace to be healthy and abundant, our minds must enter deeply into the prayer of the Church by active participation in her liturgical actions, in which she prays and worships as one with Christ, the great High Priest. This active participation necessarily implies understanding, and understanding is normally impossible without reading and meditation. Hence it is that the public and private prayer of the Christian are by no means in opposition to one another, but they complete and interpenetrate one another in a harmonious and organic union.

The full expression of a Christian life of prayer does not stop with participation in the liturgy but goes on to include extra-liturgical forms of prayer like the Rosary, as well as meditation and mental prayer. Everything that can open the spirit of man to the influence of loving faith and can inspire his heart with supernatural desires must find a place in his life of prayer. Hence it is that the Church's love for her greatest treasure, the Blessed Eucharist, does not stop at the solemn and devout celebration of Mass, but also overflows into many other public, though not liturgical, expressions of her devotion.

Also, the Church urges her faithful, and particularly her priests, to make visits to the Blessed Sacrament reserved in her tabernacles, to spend long periods of the day or night in adoration before the Blessed Sacrament exposed and enthroned upon the altar. In a word, the eucharistic life of the Church, which is publically manifested and expressed in the great liturgical Mystery, also finds expression in other forms of worship in which the devotional life of the individual Christian evolves according to the needs and attractions of each one in particular. The happy combination of liturgical prayer and extra liturgical devotion and meditation contributes to the perfect formation of the Christian as a member and replica of Christ, provided that his prayers and devotions outside the liturgy are themselves in harmony with the spirit of the liturgy and with the mind of the Church.

Nothing so effectively kills our appreciation of the Blessed Sacrament as routine. To say Mass and receive Communion automatically, to approach the sacraments in careless and distracted manner, is to take the great gifts and mysteries of God for granted, as if they were objects and facts like all the material things that enter into our lives. Under such circumstances, our faith tends to degenerate into superstition and vain observance, and indeed to become a kind of practical skepticism under the exterior appearance of pious conformity. God withdraws from our lives, and His withdrawal gradually becomes evident to everyone except ourselves. The great tragedy of our age is the fact, if one may dare to say it, that there are so many godless Christians—Christians, that is, whose religion is a matter of pure conformism and expediency. Their "faith" is little more than a permanent evasion of reality—a compromise with life. In order to avoid admitting the uncomfortable truth that they no longer have any real need for God or any vital faith in Him, they conform to the outward conduct of others like themselves. And these "believers" cling together, offering one another an apparent justification for lives that are essentially the same as the lives of their materialistic neighbors whose horizons are purely those of the world and of its transient values.

In order to counteract the danger of this spiritual paralysis, the Holy Father urges Christians to renew the fervor of their faith and to cultivate an interior life. In order to do this, we must read, we must pray, we must meditate, we must seek every possible contact with God Who sent His Son into the world to deliver men from the coldness and vanity of purely human religious forms.

Particularly stressing the value of meditation, Pope Pius XII has written:

Above all else the Church exhorts us to the practice of meditation, which raises the mind to the contemplation of heavenly things, which influences the heart with love of God and guides it on the straight path to him. *(Menti Nostrae.)*

The interior life of the ordinary Christian depends in large measure on the instruction, the example, and the prayers of the clergy. If the faithful are to enter into the liturgy, the priest himself must appreciate and understand the liturgy. And if the priest is to appreciate the great liturgical mysteries, he is obliged to meditate on them, to immerse himself in them at all times. Hence the priest soon comes to learn that, as Pope Pius XII says:

Just as the desire for priestly perfection is nourished and strengthened by daily meditation, so its neglect is the source of distaste for spiritual things.... It must therefore be stated without reservation that no other means has the unique efficacy of meditation, and that, as a consequence, its daily practice can in no wise be substituted for. *(Menti Nostrae.)*

Strengthened by meditation, the priest is able to rise to the level of his great vocation to "orient his life towards that sacrifice in which he must needs offer and immolate himself with Christ. Consequently he will not merely celebrate Holy Mass,

but will live it out intimately in his daily life."
(Menti Nostrae.) In a word, the priest must strive
after a life of sanctity which requires a "continual
communication with God." (Ibid.)

It is therefore quite natural that in his apostolic
exhortation to the priests of the world, from which
we have just taken several quotations, the Holy
Father should urge priests to spend some time *each
day* in adoration before the Blessed Sacrament:

> Before closing his day's work, the priest will betake
> himself to the Tabernacle and spend at least a little
> time there to adore Jesus in the sacrament of His love,
> to make reparation for the ingratitude of so many men,
> to enkindle in himself ever more the love of God, and
> to remain, in some sense, even during the time of re-
> pose at night, which recalls to our minds the silence of
> death, present in His Most Sacred Heart. *(Menti Nos-
> trae.)*

In response to these appeals of the Supreme Pon-
tiff, there has been formed among secular priests the
Society for Perpetual Adoration of the Blessed
Sacrament. The purpose of this society is twofold. First of all, its members spend an hour each
day in adoration before the Blessed Sacrament.
Secondly, they do so with a particular awareness
of their unity in Christ the great High Priest. It is
therefore a society in which eucharistic adoration
is carried on in the spirit of the liturgy and of the

Mass, and above all in the perspectives of the unity of the Christian priesthood in Christ.

This society came into existence in the diocese of Aosta, in the Italian Alps, during the second world war. Isolated in mountain valleys, the priests of this region united themselves in a league of prayer, in which each member took a different hour of the day or night in order that at all times there might be one of them in adoration before the Blessed Sacrament, conscious of the unity of the whole group in Christ, and praying to the Lord for his companions, for all priests and for the whole Church of God.

This splendid institution soon spread to every part of the world. Its headquarters moved from Aosta to Turin, and thence to Rome.[4] It was canonically erected by Cardinal Gilroy of Sydney in 1950.

Warmly approved by the Holy Father, the society has received as members cardinals, archbishops and bishops in every part of the world, and is attracting to its ranks an ever larger membership among priests of the secular clergy. It was enriched by indulgences in 1953.

The scope of this society is evidently wider than that of analogous groups which exist in order to

---

[4] Via Urbano VIII, No. 16. Anyone who desires more information may apply to this address.

foster devotion to the Blessed Sacrament. Here it is not only a matter of getting the members to devote themselves to the pious practice of adoration. It is above all a deepening of the Church's consciousness of the mystery of her priesthood, and of the unity of her priests in the eucharistic Lord. The love of Jesus in the Blessed Eucharist—a love which is the life and the strength of the whole movement —opens out into a deep sense of unity in Christ, which is, in fact, the purpose for which this great Sacrament was given to us by God.

A corollary to this sense of mystical unity among priests is the sense of moral obligation to a closer union with one's superiors and brother-priests by obedience and fraternal cooperation. This society is therefore not only eucharistic but "Papal"—two characteristics which are seen to be one when we realize that the society is centered upon Jesus as High Priest. Jesus lives and is present in the world through the mediation of His priests—sacramentally present in the eucharistic mystery, juridically present in the Holy Father and in the hierarchy which is united to him. Hence the essence of this particular society is centered in the inexpressible connection between the Eucharist and the priesthood.

The idea of a society of priest adorers is not entirely new. On the contrary, there has existed since 1879 a Priests' Eucharistic League, the foundation of which was inspired by the "Apostle of the Eucharist," Blessed Peter Julian Eymard. This devout nineteenth-century French priest, whose whole life was centered in his love for Jesus in the Blessed Sacrament, founded two religious orders exclusively devoted to the Eucharist, and inspired the movement of eucharistic congresses which is a notable feature of modern Catholic piety. His influence in modern eucharistic devotion has been without parallel.

The Priests' Eucharistic League has for its purpose, as Bl. Eymard himself said, "to enable priests to spend themselves more manfully for the greater glory of the Blessed Sacrament." Again, according to Bl. Eymard, it was to remind the priest that he is "primarily an adorer of the Blessed Sacrament." Hence the main object of the league is to promote a deeper interior life of union with Jesus, by longer and more frequent visits to the Blessed Sacrament, to call to arms a legion of zealous apostles of the Eucharist, priests who would be united to one another in the closest bonds of fraternal charity in Christ. Instead of a daily hour of adoration, the Eucharistic League obliges its members to make one holy hour a week, to be spent preferably in mental prayer; recitation of the breviary during this hour is discouraged by the followers of Bl. Eymard. The members also say one Mass each year for the souls of those members of the league who have gone to their rest in the Lord.

The Priests' Eucharistic League, which has members in all parts of the world, was brought to the United States in 1894 through the efforts of Father Bede Maler, O.S.B. of St. Meinrad's Abbey, and of Bishop Maes of Covington. Today the league numbers nearly 32,000 members in the U.S. and Canada; about four-fifths of the clergy in the United States belong to it.

It has already had a tremendous effect in the lives of those priests who have enrolled themselves in it. Everywhere in the world, at every moment, every day and every night, priests kneel in silence and alone before the eucharistic Christ, deeply conscious of their union with all other priests throughout the world. Wherever one of these priests is in prayer, all his brothers are praying, the whole Church is in prayer. Theirs is a most inspiring and fruitful example and the effects of their prayer are undoubtedly making themselves felt to an extent that no man can measure. But above all it is certain that each one of these priests would gladly tell his brothers in the priesthood that in his hours of eucharistic prayer he has tasted his deepest happiness outside the Holy Sacrifice of the Mass itself. For here, indeed, he has been close to the Living God, and has learned from his own experience the truth of Christ's promise: "Come to me all you who

labor and are burdened, and I will refresh you"
(Matthew 11:28).

The People's Eucharistic League, also founded
by Blessed Peter Julian Eymard, was started in the
maritime city of Marseilles. The world headquarters
were later established at Rome in the Church of Ss.
Andrew and Claude, which is served by the Fathers
of the Blessed Sacrament.[5] The principal obligation
of members is that of spending at least one hour
each month in adoration before the Blessed Sacrament, either exposed in a monstrance or enclosed in
the tabernacle. This adoration may be offered at
any hour, on any day of the month, privately or
publicly, at the convenience of the members.

Today the People's Eucharistic League is established in practically every country in the world,
and the United States alone accounts for over 700
parish centers. The official magazine of the People's
Eucharistic League in the United States is the *Sen-
tinel of the Blessed Sacrament*, issued monthly from
national headquarters. The purpose of the whole
movement is not only to encourage the interior life
of prayer in the individual, but also to promote a
deeper realization of the unity of all the faithful in

[5] The national headquarters of the People's Eucharistic
League are at St. Jean Baptiste Church, 194 East 76th Street,
New York 21. Regional offices are at 1335 West Harrison
Street, Chicago 7, and 1224 East Gold Avenue, Albuquerque,
New Mexico.

charity. Unity in Christ is the most important of all the effects of the Blessed Eucharist.

This book was written primarily as a summary of the Church's teaching on the Eucharist. It is hoped that this summary will not be found too superficial. Certain disputable theological opinions have unavoidably found their way into the treatment of the subject. The author does not intend to impose these opinions on the reader, and if they are discreetly hinted at, his only purpose is to throw greater light upon the central theme of the book, which is the intimate connection between the two mysteries of the Eucharist and of the Church. The reason we cultivate a life of prayer before the Blessed Sacrament is not only that we may ourselves become men of prayer or holier priests, but above all that we may become men of charity, peacemakers in the world, mediators between God and men, instruments of the divine priesthood of Our Lord Jesus Christ. Our mission is not only to offer Christ to the Father in the Eucharistic Sacrifice, not only to preach the word of God to all nations but, above all, by preaching and by sacrifice, to unite all men in one Mystical Body and offer them all, in Christ, to the Father.

Presumably the book will be read not only by priests and clerical students, but also by Catholics at large and even perhaps by many who are completely unacquainted with the Church's teaching about this great mystery. To these last we would only remark that these are matters which, for long centuries, the Church herself never tried to explain to those who were not her own, because such things cannot be understood without faith. To every man of good will, who reads with an open and humble mind, God will undoubtedly give whatever light he needs. But if the reader has made up his mind in advance not to accept the Catholic teaching on the Eucharist, then this is no book for him. At no point in the treatment have we permitted ourselves to indulge in apologetics. This book is not a defense of a doctrine, but a meditation on a sacred mystery.

THE LIVING BREAD

I

UNTO THE END

1. Christ's Love for Us

In writing or speaking of the Blessed Sacrament, which is the very heart and focus of the whole Christian life, there are two extremes to be avoided. On one hand we must not degrade the great sacramental mystery to the level of mere sentimentality by an abuse of pious imagination, and on the other hand we must not treat that mystery in such pure theological abstractions that we forget that it is the great sacrament of God's love for us. The simplicity of the Gospels keeps us from either of these extremes.

The Gospels tell us the sublimest mysteries of our faith in terms that are concrete and easy for any human mind to understand. Of the four evangelists, no one has given the loftiest revealed truths a more concrete embodiment than St. John the author of the Fourth Gospel. The disciple whom Jesus loved opens his account of the Last Supper and of the Passion with these deeply moving words: "Before the feast of the Passover, knowing that the hour had come for Him to pass out of the world to the Father, having loved His own who were in the world, He loved them unto the end" (John 13:1). And from these words it is immediately clear that the Sacrament and Sacrifice of the Eucharist which Jesus instituted at the Last Supper are, like His Passion and Resurrection which they perpetuate until the end of time, the ineffably perfect embodiment of His Love for us. I say "embodiment" rather than expression, because in this divine sacrament the infinite Love of God continues to be incarnate, to dwell among us in His bodily substance, hidden beneath the species of Bread and Wine.

The Christian life is nothing else but Christ living in us, by His Holy Spirit. It is Christ's love, sharing itself with us in charity. It is Christ in us, loving the Father, by His Spirit. It is Christ uniting us to our brothers by charity in the bond of this same Spirit.

Jesus often expressed His desire to share with us the mystery of His divine life. He said that He came that we might have life, and have it more abundantly (John 10:10). He came to cast that life of charity like fire upon the earth, and He longed to see it enkindled. He especially desired that He might undergo the "baptism" of His Passion and death, because He knew that by this alone He would be able to incorporate us into His mystery, and make us, with Himself, sons of God. No wonder then that He said He was "straitened," that is to say He felt like one bound and confined, like a prisoner in chains, until this baptism was accomplished. His infinite charity, imprisoned within His Sacred Heart, longed to burst out of its confinement and communicate itself to all mankind, for as God, He is substantial goodness, and the very nature of the good is to be diffusive of itself.

That is why the Church, in her liturgy, continues to apply to Christ in the Blessed Eucharist those words which Jesus spoke to the suffering men of His time: "Come to me all you who labor and are burdened, and I will refresh you"[1] (Matth. 11:28). For in the Eucharist the Christ of the Last Supper still breaks bread with His disciples, still washes their feet to show them that unless He abase Himself and minister to them they can have no part in Him (John 13:8). In the Eucharist, He still blesses the sacred chalice and hands it to those He loves. There is only one difference. At the Last Supper, Christ had not yet suffered, died and risen. Now, at our daily Mass, the Christ Who enters silently and invisibly to become present in the midst of His disciples is the Christ Who sits in glory at the right

---

[1] Invitatory, Feast of Corpus Christi, Monastic Breviary.

hand of God the Father in heaven. It is Christ the immortal King and Conqueror. It is Christ Who, having died once for us, "dieth now no more" (Rom. 6:9). At the same time, He comes to us in all the simplicity, the poverty, the obscurity which we have learned, from the Gospels, to associate with His Incarnation.

In rising from death, Jesus lost nothing of His humanity. Ascending in glory into the inaccessible mystery of the Godhead, His throne, He did not cease to love us with the same human tenderness and completeness which St. John describes in three simple words: "unto the end." The Blessed Eucharist opens up to us the depths of meaning which those three words contain.

In saying that Jesus loved His own "unto the end," the evangelist is not merely telling us that Our Savior loved us to the very end of His earthly life, that He loved us so much that He died for us. Jesus said: "Greater love than this no man hath, that a man lay down his life for his friends" (John 15:13). And yet Jesus Himself has done more than lay down His life for us. He has loved us with a love that cannot be confined by the ordinary boundaries of human life. In giving us the Eucharist as a "memorial" of His passion, death and resurrection, He has made present, for all time, the love with which he died for us. More than that, He has made the Passion itself present in mystery. And He Him-

self, Who knew and saw us by His divine fore-
knowledge when He blessed bread in the Cenacle
and when He took up His Cross, wills to be substantially present in the Eucharist, to know us and
love us, to share His presence and love with us
sacramentally until the end of time.

Now this desire of Christ was far more than an
expression of the purest human tenderness. It is not
merely as a gesture of fond affection that He remains with us in the Eucharist. His divine work
was accomplished, objectively, when He breathed
forth His soul on the Cross. But, as He said through
the lips of the Psalmist (Ps. 15:10) there would be
no value in His Blood if it went down into corrup-
tion. He consecrated Himself as a sacrificial offering (John 17:19) in order that we might be
"sanctified in truth" (idem.). If He comes to us
in the Blessed Sacrament, He comes with work to
do: not in Himself, but in us. And what is this
work? John tells us, in the great eucharistic chapter
of the Fourth Gospel: "This is the work of God,
that you believe in Him whom He has sent" (John
6:29). And if we know the Gospels, we realize that
the word "believe" here implies far more than a
simple intellectual assent to revealed truth. It means
the wholehearted acceptance not only of the Gospel
message but of the very person of Christ. It means
doing the works of Christ, for "he who believes in
me, the works that I do he also shall do" (John

14:12). It means loving Christ, and by virtue of that love receiving the Spirit of Christ into our hearts. It means keeping His commandments, particularly loving one another (John 14:21). It means realizing that Christ is in the Father, and we in Christ, and Christ in us (John 14:20).

In a word, the work Christ does in the world, through the action of His Spirit, through His Church, and through His holy sacraments, is the work of incorporating and transforming us into Himself by charity. This is the work above all of the Holy Eucharist.

Now in the reception of the sacraments, it is of course first of all necessary that we believe in Christ, Who sanctifies us through the sacraments. We must be baptized Christians. We must live according to our baptismal vows, and renounce sin. We must consecrate ourselves to God and to His divine charity. We must live unselfishly, that is to say, we must find our own fulfillment in loving God and other men. But in order that the sacraments may produce their full effect in us, in order particularly that our eucharistic life may be really a *life* and not a mere outward formality, we must strive to increase not only our appreciation of the sacramental mystery itself, but also our understanding of the love of Christ Who is present and Who acts on us in the Sacrament.

These two are simply different aspects of the

same thing, which is Christ's love for us. On the one hand, the marvelous reality of Christ's sacramental presence, a mystery of God's wisdom and power, bathes and purifies our intelligence with a clean light that awakens the depths of our will to a love beyond all human affection. On the other hand His love for us awakens in our hearts a spiritual instinct to love Him in return, and by this love we come to know God.

Love for God is the deepest fulfillment of the powers implanted by God in our human nature which He has destined for union with Himself. In loving Him, we discover not only the inner meaning of truths which we would otherwise never be able to understand, but we also find our true selves in Him. The charity which is stirred up in our hearts by the Spirit of Christ acting in the depths of our being makes us begin to be the persons He has destined us to be in the inscrutable designs of His Providence. Moved by the grace of Christ we begin to discover and to know Christ Himself as a friend knows a friend—by the inner sympathy and understanding which friendship alone can impart. This loving knowledge of God is one of the most important fruits of eucharistic communion with God in Christ.

St. Paul, in his Epistles, repeatedly sums up the whole meaning of the mature Christian life. Writing to the Ephesians, he tells them how important it is for them "to be strengthened with power through His Spirit unto the progress of the inner man and to have Christ dwelling through faith in your hearts, so that being rooted and grounded in love you may be able to comprehend with all the saints ... and to know Christ's love which surpasses knowledge, in order to be filled with all the fullness of God" (Ephesians 3:16-19). Here in a few words we see something of the purpose of Holy Communion, considered as the summit of the life of faith and of the sacraments. Nourished by the Gospel message, by the life of fraternal solidarity in Christ, by liturgical and private prayer, the Christian finds that his inner life reaches its highest peak of ever increasing intensity when, in his eucharistic communion with the Lord, he is united directly and sacramentally to the Incarnate Word. In Communion, he is not only penetrated through and through by the mystical fire of Christ's charity, but rests in an immediate contact with the very Person of the Word Incarnate. In such union, how can one whose charity remains vigilant in the darkness of faith fail to gain a deeper and more intimate knowledge of the very soul of Jesus? This love, this knowledge of the Lord, at once the purest and most secret effect of Holy Communion, is without doubt one which has a very great importance in the eyes of Christ Himself. For His intention in instituting the Blessed Sacrament was to give us this lofty and mysterious participation in His own divine life. "Amen, amen I say to you, unless you eat the flesh of the Son of Man and drink His Blood, you shall not have life in you" (John 6:54). But it is quite clear that this life of which Jesus speaks is in the highest sense the life of the spirit, not merely the life of the flesh. Communion is a contact with His Spirit Who "gives life; the flesh profits nothing." The very words of this doctrine are, He says, "spirit and life" (John 6:64). But the most perfect fulfillment of this life which begins with faith, is the contemplation of God. Our growth in life is a growth in knowledge and love of God, in Jesus Christ. "This is eternal life that they may know Thee, the only true God, and Him whom Thou hast sent, Jesus Christ" (John 17:3).

2. Our Response

If we are Christians in all truth, we will desire to grow and develop in this eucharistic life which is nothing else but the Christian life in all its perfection. We will seek to realize more and more what it means to receive Christ sacramentally and have Him living in us, what it means to be members of His Mystical Body, united to one another in Him by our communions. We will pray for a deeper and deeper understanding of the great mystery which sums up the whole plan of God for His world, and the whole mission of Christ in the world: the recapitulation of all in Christ, the work of charity which transforms us all in Him so that we are one in Him as He is one with the Father and the Holy Spirit.

Our communions are more truly and more perfectly what they are called when they are a sharing in the divine life of contemplation and love which Christ lives in the Blessed Trinity. Our communions are most fruitful when, besides increasing our charity for other men and deepening our faith, they bring us a more intimate and purer knowledge of the mystery of Christ in Whom we are all one.

There are three chief ways in which this can be done. The first is by active participation in the liturgy. The second by a more profound and purer life of charity, as the outcome of our participation in the Mass. The third is by meditation and adoration and contemplative prayer before the Blessed Sacrament. Of these three the first two are absolutely essential, and the third is very important.

These three ways are simply aspects of our eucharistic communion. The most perfect participation in the sacrifice of the Mass is to receive Communion at a Mass which one has followed intelligently and actively through all its principal parts. Our life of charity is, or should be, the prolongation and expression of our communions. It testifies to the reality of our oneness in Christ, which is signified and effected by the very Sacrament which we receive and which is one of the chief fruits of sacramental communion. Jesus, in giving to us His own Body in Mystery, makes us one Body in Himself, members one of another.

Eucharistic adoration, and mental prayer in silence before the tabernacle, provide another fruitful way of prolonging our communion. All these three ways of developing our eucharistic life are necessary. They complete one another. Adoration and mental prayer without any interest in the Mass would be a perversion of the Christian spirit. Fraternal charity and good works, even united with the Mass and flowing from it, might still lead to a deviation from the right road if they did not imply some moments of silent thanksgiving after Communion, and of meditation and adoration before the tabernacle.

At the present time the tendency is to stress our participation in the action of the Holy Sacrifice, and the overflow of our eucharistic life in apostolic action or other works of charity. This emphasis is excellent. The need for it has been felt for a long time and it is most necessary in the hour of crisis in which we find ourselves. The emphasis on eucharistic adoration has long been popular, and it was one of the characteristic features of Christian devotion in the age that has been brought to an end by two world wars. But are we to think that it is merely a passing fashion, something that will gradually drop out of existence as the full meaning of the central action of the Church's liturgical life regains its full prominence?

In any case, our response to Christ's love for us in the Blessed Eucharist is to live a full and well-integrated eucharistic life. In such a life, communion, adoration, fraternal charity, and active participation in the liturgy will not be seen as separate and unrelated "practices." They will be drawn together in one supremely relevant focus upon the central Mystery of our faith—our sharing in the death and resurrection of Jesus Christ. When we really begin to grasp the meaning of this great Mystery, we will no longer be preoccupied with an apparent contradiction between liturgical and non-liturgical devotion to Christ in the Blessed Sacrament. One will flow naturally from the other, and each will retain its proper place in relation to the other. The so-called "extra-liturgical" devotions to the Blessed Sacrament will be seen as a fruitful prolongation of the liturgy, and our meditation before the tabernacle will help us to enter more deeply into the truth of Christ's actual presence under the sacramental veils—a presence without which the ritual mystery of the Mass could not be accomplished.

If Christ is not sacramentally present in the Eucharist, then the Mass is no longer anything but a ceremony, a pious commemoration of a past event. If Christ is not actually present in the consecrated Host, then the priest is nothing but a preacher, not a man set apart by God to offer sacrifice. Indeed, if Christ is not really and substantially present in the Blessed Eucharist, then the doctrine of the Mystical Body of Christ, the Church, also loses its meaning and becomes nothing more than a metaphor: for it is the Sacramental Christ Who is the Head and support of the Mystical Body. It is the Eucharist that unites us in one Body to Christ our Head: "Because the bread is one, we though many are one body, all of us who partake of one bread" (I Cor. 10:17).

It is necessary that we know and love Christ, as He really is. Now the real Christ is the *whole* Christ, the Mystical Christ, the Head and the Members. The real Christ is also the Head whom the members must know if they are to be His members. This glorious Head and King of mankind and High Priest of the One Church is enthroned in the majesty of His divine power in heaven. But He is also present under the veils of the sacrament that is revered and adored in our tabernacles. And the real Christ is also the Christ who was poor, who labored and suffered for us on earth, who died for us on the Cross. This suffering Christ is present in the Blessed Sacrament, not in the same way as His glorified Body is present, but by virtue of the fact that in His life and Passion He foreknew and foresaw all that would take place in the world around Him in the ages to come when this sacrament would be adored, and praised and loved by men.

When we seek Christ in the Blessed Sacrament we must then seek Him as He really is. We must recognize Him as the Redeemer Who has suffered for us, as King Who reigns over us, as the Life who lives in all our fellow Christians. We are free to emphasize any one of these aspects of the Living Christ Who is before us in the Tabernacle, as long as we remember that one of them is more essential than the others. If we would answer the question Who is present in the Blessed Sacrament, we must say: the glorious Christ who reigns in heaven. This is the answer of the Catholic faith. This glorious Christ is, indeed, the Christ Who has suffered. But though His sufferings are still present to Him, it is not strictly speaking the suffering Christ Who is present in the Blessed Sacrament. And though He lives by grace in all the members of His Mystical Body, it is not the Mystical Body of Christ (in the modern sense) that is present on the altar.

The best way to unite all these three conceptions of Christ in one (for they are in fact all one in Him Who is present there before us) is to realize that the glorious Christ Who comes to us hidden under the sacramental species is the same Christ Who, having redeemed and sanctified us, will be our everlasting joy in heaven. Our life of eucharistic prayer and adoration is, in fact, the beginning of that contemplation of God in Christ which will be our whole life when we enter into His glory.

When we grasp the meaning of this truth we will understand that although we may be praying alone in a small, dark, empty church, praying with difficulty, dry and distracted, we are in fact not only united by love to Christ in His Passion, not only prostrate in adoration before Christ in glory, but we are one body with all those who are praying in different places and at different times. All we who pray before the tabernacle, and even those who cannot pray there, but must give themselves to various duties for the love of Christ, are in fact mysteriously united in a profound and secret "liturgy"; an act of worship offered to God by Christ (though not officially) in His mystical Body.

Our contemplation is a worship that anticipates the vision and the praise of heaven. Though we may hardly feel anything of the kind, we must realize that the meditation which prolongs our Mass and Communion is also a mysterious reproduction on earth of the great chorus of adoration that goes up even now in heaven before God.

What do we see before us in the empty church?

A little altar, a poorly furnished sanctuary, a couple of statues of doubtful artistic worth, a cracked wall darkened by the smoke of candles and stained by dampness? A tabernacle that no one would consider worthy to be the dwelling of a doll, let alone of a king? But no, that is not what we see. Let us look rather through the eyes of St. John:

And I saw, and behold, in the midst of the throne and of the four living creatures, and in the midst of the elders, a Lamb standing as though slain, having seven horns and seven eyes, which are the seven spirits of God sent forth into all the earth ... And the four living creatures and the twenty four elders fell down before the Lamb, having each a harp and golden bowls full of incense, which are the prayers of the saints. And they sing a new canticle, saying: "Worthy art thou to take the scroll, and open its seals; for thou wast slain and hast redeemed us for God with thy blood, out of every tribe and tongue and people and nation, and hast made them for our God a kingdom and priests, and they shall reign over the earth (Apocalypse 5:6-10).

In that great act of worship, we have our place. Poor though we may be, we are the members of Christ, and therefore our prayers contribute something to the cloud of incense which goes up from the golden bowls. We are in the presence of the Living Christ. Our prayers are united to the prayers of His saints.

II

DO THIS IN MEMORY OF ME

1. The Christian Sacrifice

The Eucharist is the Christian sacrifice. It is the "clean oblation" which was prophesied by Malachias, which is offered everywhere on earth, replacing the ancient sacrifices which could not of themselves achieve any supernatural effect and which were, consequently, doomed to remain frustrated except in so far as they were types that foreshadowed the one true sacrifice.

In the Eucharist Jesus Christ, through the instrumentality of the priest, makes present the oblation and immolation by which He offered Himself to God on the Cross. In the mystery of this liturgical action the Church unites herself with the divine High Priest and offers her members to God with Him. Receiving the Eucharist in communion, the faithful complete their act of homage to God, which is at the same time Christ's eternal act of homage. They renew and deepen their supernatural relationship with God, receiving from Him an increase of the divine life of charity which He pours out upon all those who have become, in Christ, His adopted sons.

Although the precise subject of this book is not the sacrifice of the Mass, it is impossible not to speak of the Mass when we speak of the Eucharist as Sacrament. The Sacrament and Sacrifice of the Eucharist are inseparable. The Real Presence of Christ in the Host is the necessary and immediate consequence of transubstantiation. But the purpose of transubstantiation is first of all to make Christ present on the altar in a state of sacrifice or immolation, by the separate consecration of the two species of Bread and Wine. At the same time the sacrifice cannot be completed without these consecrated elements being received in communion at least by the celebrating priest. Finally, the consecrated Host is kept in reserve in the tabernacle in order that the sick and others who cannot receive at the time of Mass may be able to receive the Body of Our Lord at some other time and thus have their share in the sacrifice of Christ. What we adore in our visits to the Blessed Sacrament is therefore Jesus Christ Himself, permanently present in the Host which was consecrated in the Holy

Sacrifice and which will eventually be received in Communion.

St. Paul makes it very clear that the New Testament considers the death of Christ on the Cross, ratified by His subsequent Resurrection, as a sacrifice. Indeed it is the only sacrifice perfectly acceptable to God. What do we mean by a sacrifice "acceptable to God"? Does God need our sacrifices? St. Irenaeus answers: "Sacrifice is called acceptable to God not because God needs sacrifice from us, but because he who offers sacrifice is glorified himself in that which he offers, if his gift is accepted";[1] and St. Irenaeus goes on to explain that the gift that is really acceptable to God is our love for one another, which is signified by the Eucharist and is the principal effect of this great Sacrament. When we love one another, God truly receives the Blessed Eucharist from us as a pleasing gift from His friends, and it gives Him the glory which we owe him.

Again St. Irenaeus says: "God has no need of those things which belong to us, but we, on the other hand, have need to offer sacrifice to God ... and God Who has need of nothing, takes our good works to Himself in order to give us a reward from the treasury of His own gifts. ... So although He does not need sacrifices from us, He wishes us

---

[1] See St. Irenaeus, *Adversus Haereses*, IV, 18.

to offer sacrifice, lest our lives be without fruit."

These two quotations remind us that the Fathers wished to assert the infinite transcendence of God and to guard against any thought of confusing Him with the gods of the pagans who demanded sacrifices because they needed them. The Fathers also stressed the fact that God is glorified by the Sacrifice of Jesus not only because that sacrifice is infinitely perfect and pure in itself, but because it is a means by which God shows His love for us and thus manifests His goodness in our lives. Jesus Himself made this quite clear in His High Priestly prayer, when he said: "Father, glorify thy Son, that thy Son may glorify thee ... I am glorified in them (whom thou hast given me) ... For them do I sanctify myself that they may be sanctified in truth. ... And the glory which Thou hast given me I have given them; that they may be one as we also are one ... I will that where I am they also may be, that they may see my glory" (John 17:1, 10, 19, 22, 24).

In this teaching of Jesus we can find the four ends of the sacrifice of the Mass inextricably interwoven with one another. The first and most important function of this Holy Sacrifice is to give infinite glory to God and the second is closely related to this: it must give Him a perfect return of praise and thanksgiving for all His goodness to men. Then it must offer Him a worthy propitiation for all our sins, and obtain for us not only the forgiveness of our offenses and of the punishment due to them, but also all the graces, all the temporal and spiritual aids which we need in order to carry out His will on earth and come to union with Him in heaven. Now it is true that God is glorified by all the effects and fruits of the Holy Sacrifice, but we must emphasize the fact that before everything else, the infinite objective value of the Divine Victim offered to God gives Him an infinite glory and adoration irrespective of the dispositions of those who offer the sacrifice and apart from the fruits which they may be able to receive from it. It is therefore primarily because of the Person of the Victim, the Word Incarnate, that this sacrifice is above all acceptable to God. All the other fruits and effects of this Holy Sacrifice flow from this one great truth, that the immolation of Jesus Himself, the Son of God, is infinitely pleasing to Him and gives Him all the glory which is His due.

After describing in some detail the imperfect sacrifices of the Old Law, St. Paul goes on to contrast with them the sacrifice of Christ in which their typology is finally revealed and explained. Christ is the true High Priest, the priest of that "new covenant" which has made the old alliance obsolete and has replaced it (Hebrews 8:13). In His one true sacrifice, Christ has offered to the Father in heaven not the blood of sheep or goats but His own Body and Blood. In so doing, He enters not into a "tabernacle made with hands" as did the Jewish high priest when he went into the holy of holies to offer the blood of the victim to God, but into the uncreated sanctuary of heaven (Hebrews 9:11). The effect of the sacrifice of Christ is to cleanse our souls of sin and to bring us once again into the friendship of God: "how much more will the blood of Christ, who through the Holy Spirit offered Himself unblemished unto God, cleanse your conscience from dead works to serve the living God?" (Hebrews 9:14). "Once for all at the end of the ages He has appeared for the destruction of sin by the sacrifice of Himself" (idem 26).

This sacrifice, consummated once for all on Calvary, is represented and renewed in the sacrifice of the Eucharist. Indeed, at the Last Supper Jesus offered this Holy Sacrifice which was to be consummated the following day in the shedding of His Most Precious Blood, and since that first Mass in the Upper Room He has made present His sacrifice everywhere day after day, through the medium of His priests.

Hence the Mass itself is a true sacrifice in the strict sense of the word forming but one sacrifice with that of Calvary.

It is not merely a sacrifice in the sense of an act of praise, or of thanksgiving, a *sacrificium laudis*, but the oblation and immolation of a victim for sin,

Who is Christ Himself. Therefore this sacrifice is something more than a prayer for pardon. It is infinite propitiation for all the offenses that have ever been committed against God. And each time the Mass is offered, the fruits of our Redemption are poured out anew upon our souls. By uniting ourselves with the sacred rite of the Mass, and above all by receiving Holy Communion, we enter into the sacrifice of Christ. We mystically die with the divine Victim and rise again with Him to a new life in God. We are freed from our sins, we are once again pleasing to God, and we receive grace to follow Him more generously in the life of charity and fraternal union which is the life of His Mystical Body.

Only in the light of this doctrine of the eucharistic life as a full participation in the sacrifice of Christ can we understand the moral and mystical theology of St. Paul. "For Christ our passover has been sacrificed," he says. "Therefore let us keep festival not with the old leaven of malice and wickedness, but with the unleavened bread of sincerity and truth" (I Corinthians 5:7-8). "If you have risen with Christ, seek the things that are above where Christ is seated at the right hand of God. Mind the things that are above, not the things that are on earth. For you have died and your life is hidden with Christ in God. When Christ your life shall appear, then you too will appear with Him in glory" (Colossians 3:1-4). As for this last thought, we remember that St. John makes an explicit connection between eucharistic communion and resurrection at the last day. "He who eats my flesh and drinks my blood has life everlasting and I will raise him up on the last day" (John 6:54).

The Mass is then the Passover, the *Pascha* of the New Law. In the blood of the divine Victim we are not only delivered from the avenging angel that struck the first-born of Egypt, not only saved from the power of Pharao, but we pass, with Christ, "out of this world to the Father" (John 13:1).

The sacrifice of the Mass is therefore the renewal of the Sacrifice of Calvary. The same High Priest, Jesus Christ, offers the same Victim—Himself. The only difference is in the manner in which the sacrifice is offered. On Calvary, Jesus laid down His life in suffering, shedding His Blood for the sins of men. Risen from the dead, He dies no more. At the altars of His sacrifice, He Himself speaks when the consecrating priest utters the words which effect the miracle of transubstantiation. They are the same words which Jesus first pronounced over Bread and Wine at the Last Supper. "This is My Body" (Luke 22:19). "This is My Blood of the new covenant" (Mark 14:24). In the Mass Jesus fulfills His promise that He would drink of the fruit of this vine "new with you in the Kingdom of my Father" (Matthew 26:29).

When we go to the altar to receive the Host from the hands of the priest, we are mystically present at that Holy Supper in which with His own hands Jesus broke bread, which had been changed into His Sacred Body, and distributed it to His Apostles. By virtue of our participation in this sacrificial banquet, we enter in all reality, though still sacramentally and mystically, into the sacrifice of the Cross. Sharing in the fruits of that Most Holy Sacrifice by our communion, we are identified with the divine Victim and by that very fact pass with Him from the world of sin into the mercy of the Father and the light of His divine favor.

Here is how one of the Fathers of the Church, St. Cyril of Jerusalem, in the fourth century, describes the sacrifice of the Mass:

Then, having sanctified ourselves by spiritual hymns (the *trisagion*) we call upon the merciful God to send His Holy Spirit upon the gifts lying before Him (the unconsecrated species of bread and wine), that He may make the bread the Body of Christ and the wine the Blood of Christ for whatsoever the Holy Ghost has touched is sanctified and changed. Then after the spiritual sacrifice is perfected ... we entreat God for the peace of the Church, for the tranquillity of the world ... in a word for all who stand in need of succor we all supplicate and offer this sacrifice. ... We commemorate also those who have fallen asleep ... believing that it will be a very great advantage to the souls

... When we offer to Him our supplications for those who have fallen asleep ... we offer up Christ, sacrificed for our sins, propitiating our merciful God both for them and for ourselves.[2]

2. *Worship*

The modern world is no longer very familiar with the notion of ritual sacrifice. A few words on the nature of sacrifice are needed to show that the Eucharist is a sacrifice in the highest and purest sense. In fact, it should not be thought of in comparison with any other sacrificial rite.

In general, sacrifice is an act by which man satisfies the law of his nature which demands that he express outwardly, in a significant act, his interior submission to and dependance upon a "numinous" power. The idea of sacrifice is incomprehensible if we fail to see it as the response to a deep religious sense of the sacred, the "holy." If it is not an expression of at least an inchoate awareness of the reality of the divine, sacrifice remains nothing but an

---

[2] St. Cyril of Jerusalem, *Catechesis Mystagogica*, 5.

empty gesture, even on the natural plane. And because man's response to the holy is so tenuous and
inconstant, ritual sacrifice on the natural level does
tend, precisely, to degenerate into vain observance.
This is a sign that the outward action no longer
corresponds to the interior and spiritual realities
which it is supposed to express, or else that the interior response of the worshipper itself has been fal-
sified and corrupted in some way that has perhaps
not been realized by the moral consciousness of the
offerer.

The normal psychological response to an awareness of a holy power is submission and worship.
Sacrifice is the most powerful outward expression of
interior worship. It is the offering, the consecration,
the "setting apart" of some object that is precious
and necessary to ourselves, so that it is no longer
ours but belongs to the Holy One. The normal way
of "setting apart" an object is to destroy it in a way
that implies that it is being "given" to God while
being renounced by ourselves. The higher and
purer the religion, the deeper is the meaning of the
sacrificial act. If a person has a low idea of God he
will also have a low idea of sacrifice, and in that
event his sacrifice will have something of the character of a "deal" with the divinity, who is imagined
to need and desire things that men also need and
desire. The divinity is thus considered as someone
just a little more powerful than man, but with the

same instincts and appetites. In such circumstances, religion is scarcely separable from superstition.

The higher we rise in the religious scale, and the more spiritual our notion of God becomes, the more we realize the infinite distance between Him and ourselves. We are more and more aware of His utter transcendence, yet at the same time we cannot escape the realization of His all-pervading immanence. In the Old Testament, animal sacrifices were offered to the Living God because the minds of the people were still prone to idolatrous worship, and they had to have something that would make a vivid impression and keep them from drifting away to the exciting rites of the earth gods of Canaan. But the prophets of Israel did not hesitate to rebuke the complacent Levitical priesthood for their trust in these sacrifices. Isaias prepared the way for the new covenant when he said, in the name of Yahveh:

To what purpose do you offer me the multitude of your victims saith the Lord. I am full, I desire not holocausts of rams and fat of fatlings and blood of calves and lambs and buck goats. . . . Offer sacrifice no more in vain. Incense is an abomination to me. The new moons and sabbaths and other festivals I will not abide, your assemblies are wicked. My soul hateth your new moons and your solemnities: they are become troublesome to me. I am weary of bearing them. And when you stretch forth your hands I will turn away my eyes from you: and when you multiply prayer I will not hear, for your hands are full of blood. (Isaias 1:11-15).

Here we begin to see the development of an idea of interior sacrifice in which man offers *himself* to God instead of offering victims. And, as the prophet's context explains, this interior offering of ourselves consists in justice and mercy and goodness to other men, acts of virtue by which our soul itself, the highest part of our being, is consecrated to God by good and spiritual intentions. Nevertheless this interior sacrifice still demands to be expressed outwardly in a ritual action, because man, being a creature with body and soul, needs exterior rites. They can do much for his interior and spiritual life. Besides, man is a social being and sacrifice is also a social act, a recognition, on the part of society itself, of certain spiritual values which are the *sine qua non* of our dedication to God both as individuals and as a group.

At the present time, the idea of sacrifice that prevails even among certain Christians leads them to emphasize the moral and subjective parts of this great act. A sacrifice tends to be regarded as the performance of a difficult act, requiring courage and detachment, and bearing fruit in an increase of personal merit. This may be true as far as it goes, but we must not forget that the essential note of sacrifice lies in its objective orientation to God. It is not something difficult that we do for ourselves or for other people. It is not something difficult that we do for God merely in order to improve our relations with Him. It is an act of worship *strictly due* to God, an expression, a manifestation, a "witness" to the reality of our position with regard to Him and therefore a testimony to His infinite sanctity and goodness and power. In a word, sacrifice is not essentially an act of temperance or fortitude which makes us subjectively more holy (although in the broad sense it may well be that too). It is above all an act of justice, of worship. It is a grateful acknowledgment of reality, an acceptance of our place as creatures who belong to their Creator and who must use their freedom to know and to fulfill the destiny He has planned for them. It is an acknowledgment of sin, and an attempt at reparation. It is a plea for pardon. It gives God glory.

3. Atonement

It would be a grave error to construct an *a priori* theory of sacrifice, based on notions discovered in the natural order, and then attempt to justify the sacrifice of the Mass on the grounds that it fits a common definition applicable to all sacrifices. The Sacrifice of the Eucharist is in a class entirely by itself, and though it has certain features in common with other sacrifices, this is not because it has borrowed anything from the natural order. It is rather that natural sacrifices, by the fact that they were commanded by the God of nature, reflected something hidden in the mind of God which He intended to manifest more perfectly in the one true sacrifice which the Son of God Himself would offer to the Father.

It would appear, however, that one common element in all sacrifices is the striving for reconciliation with God that is Atonement. The purity of a sacrifice corresponds, in fact, to the purity of the notion of reconciliation which it implies. And this in turn depends on the conception of alienation from God which makes us want to be reconciled with Him.

To aid us in understanding our need for reconciliation with God, we may distinguish between a contrite sense of sin and a feeling of guilt. The distinction between the two may not always be clear, because they sometimes overlap. They belong to some extent together. However, by a contrite sense of sin I mean a true and healthy thing, and by the feeling of guilt I mean something that tends to be false and consequently pathological.

Both these drives make us feel alienated from the sources of our life. They manifest two different reactions to a realization that we are not what we ought to be. What I call a sense of sin implies the sorrowful recognition that we have used our freedom against ourselves and against God. That we have made ourselves into something that we were not meant to be, and have consequently disobeyed the voice of God's truth speaking in our inmost conscience.

I also mean by a sense of sin a perception of actual fact, not an illusion. It is the indication that we really are, in fact, alienated from the truth and from God's love. It shows us at least to some extent the cause of this alienation. The contrite sense of sin moves us to seek pardon, and reconciliation with God by a new adaptation to reality. It makes us therefore desire to *change ourselves*. It drives us to become new beings. And it turns to God hoping that He Who made us will remake us according to the truth which He knows better than we do, because He Himself is that Truth.

A feeling of guilt, on the other hand, may well arise from the perception of an actual moral disorder in our lives. But in the harmful sense which I am giving to the term, it is something quite different from the sense of sin. In the first place, it implies no efficacious desire to change, no real drive to become healthy. It does not seek the truth, only the undisputed possession of its own illusions. Hence it is morbidly servile, and will not face reality. The man who suffers from a sense of guilt certainly does not want to *feel guilty*. But he does not want to *be innocent*. He wants to do what he thinks he must not do, without the pain of worrying about the consequences. Now very often this feeling of guilt is itself an illusion. It is a matter of common experience that one can "feel" much more defiled and degraded by a fault that is objectively trivial than by a very serious sin, and the emotion of shame is not always a reliable indication of moral offense. On the contrary, a man may sometimes feel ashamed of something which ought, in fact, to be a reason for self-congratulation.

The kind of "sacrifice" that is prompted by this particular feeling of guilt will therefore be a futile and superstitious act, the main purpose of which is not to please God but simply to allay anxiety. God may indeed be considered as the one to whom the sacrifice is offered, but He will then be seen only under the disfigurement of our own projected fears. The more intense the feeling of guilt, and the deeper the conflict in which the guilt itself is rooted, the more violent, bloody and perverse will be the nature of the sacrifice.

The history of our own time has been made by dictators whose characters, often transparently easy to read, have been full of repressed guilt, self-hatred and feelings of inferiority. They have managed to enlist the support of solid masses of men moved by the same repressed drives as themselves. The wars they have waged with one another have been the sacrifice which the masses, degraded by totalitarianism, have offered up in fanatical self-idolatry, which never completely manages to assuage the nausea brought about by self-hatred.

This digression on the inexpressible moral evils of our time has been necessary. To such a mentality as we have been describing, the Eucharist cannot possibly have much meaning. Certainly it cannot reveal its deep significance to us unless we desire objective reconciliation with God, rather than the mere allaying of our own subjective sense of guilt and anxiety. Logically, this would require us to speak of baptism before going any further with the Eucharist, but that would take us far afield. It is sufficient to say that the healing effect of the sacraments of baptism, confirmation and penance (and, in the appropriate cases, of extreme unction) have been given us to repair and resist this great evil of sin in our souls and to adapt us objectively to supernatural reality.

The meaning of the sacrifice of the Eucharist is only accessible to one who realizes who God is, what sin is, who we are, who Christ is and what He has done for us. This presupposes a spiritual formation which is not possible without the gift of faith. At the same time the sacramental life of the Church promotes and furthers the life of faith. Faith and the sacraments are two channels by which the merits of the Passion of Christ are applied to our souls. In the words of St. Thomas, a spiritual power goes forth from the Body of Christ, hypostatically united to the Word. This power works on our souls if we make contact with Him, and the contact is established by "faith and the sacraments of faith."[3]

In another section, St. Thomas reminds us that the Eucharist not only applies to our souls the merits of the Passion, but contains Christ Himself Who suffered for us. It is clear that in the sacrifice of the Mass we come into the closest possible contact with the Body of Christ, the author of all sanctification, in the very act by which He takes away the sins of the world. This is truly an objective Atonement.

And what is the peculiar source of the fruitfulness of this sacrifice? The infinite value of the Body and Blood of Christ and the infinite power of His charity. To begin with, He is a divine person, the Word of God. The value of His actions is infinite, for they are divine. But since they are performed by a *man*—a human nature united to God—and for

---

[3] Passio Christi, licet sit corporalis, habet tamen spiritualem virtutem ex divinitate unita: et ideo per spiritualem contactum efficaciam sortitur, scilicet per fidem et fidei sacramentum. *Summa Theologica*, III, Q.48, a.6, ad 2.

men, they are all acceptable to God as an offering of humanity itself. In Christ, mankind becomes once again supernaturally pleasing to God and capable of union with Him.

The less realization we have of the reality of God, the less we feel any need of reconciliation with Him. The objective idea of sacrifice as an act of worship due to God in justice is sooner lost than the subjective sense of the value of "sacrifices" which demand moral fortitude and which make us more perfect and more virtuous. Even among Catholics who meditate on their faith, the Mass is often regarded as primarily the exhibition of the virtues and sufferings that one may see in the Passion of Christ rather than as an act of worship and objective satisfaction offered by Him to His Father. The virtues and sufferings of Christ are by no means to be ignored, but neither must we forget that the objective value of His sacrifice—and this objective value is infinite in itself—comes from the fact that His offering was acceptable to God, and was received by God as an "odor of sweetness." In other words, the most important thing of all about the Sacrifice of Calvary and about the Mass is not the fact that it is an expression of sublime heroism in Christ, but above all that it is *pleasing to God.* Failure to appreciate this fact would be evidence that our spirituality is not founded on a desire to please God as much as on a desire to be heroic ourselves. And this can easily corrupt its way into pure narcissism and the desire to make an exhibition of ourselves in the eyes of men.

Let us therefore cultivate a deep appreciation both of the objective and of the subjective elements in the sacrifice of the Mass. But let us above all put first things first. The Mass is the greatest of all acts of worship, not only because it is the most sanctifying for ourselves but also and above all because it gives the most glory to God and pleases Him more than anything else on earth. Of course the two things are really one in the sense that God is most pleased by the act in which He has decreed to show His mercy to us in the most efficacious manner—and the Mass is what does this.

The Resurrection of Christ from the dead was the sign of God's acceptance of His sacrifice, and therefore the more objective our appreciation of the Mass, the more we will be aware that, as the priest says right after the Consecration, it is a memorial of the Passion, Resurrection and Ascension of Christ. Far from dividing our attention and "distracting" us from the great redemptive fact of Christ's death on the Cross, this broader outlook gives us an even deeper realization of the power and meaning of the Cross. For, as St. Paul says, it was because Jesus became obedient even unto the death of the Cross that "God also has exalted Him and bestowed upon Him a Name which is above every other name, so that at the Name of Jesus, every knee should bend, of those in heaven, on earth and under the earth" (Philippians 2:9).

The liturgy teaches us best of all how to keep a perfect balance between the objective and subjective aspects of the Mass, and preserves a perfect sense of proportion in the harmony of ritual and asceticism which is proper to the Christian life. One has but to consult a few of the prayers of the Missal, particularly the secret prayers of the more ancient Masses, to realize this great truth.

The sacrifice of the Mass sanctifies our Lenten fast, for example, and gives it a deeper, more interior, more spiritual character.[4] By the strong power of this sacrifice we are brought purified to the source of its action—*Haec sacrificia nos, omnipotens Deus, potenti virtute mundatos, ad suum faciant puriores venire principium.*[5] From this sacrifice we receive "eternal remedies"[6] for all our weaknesses and sins. The action of the sacrifice makes us also spiritual victims worthy to be offered to God.[7] In a word, "each time this saving Victim is offered up, the work of our Redemption is carried out."[8]

---

[4] Praesentibus sacrificiis, quaesumus Domine, jejunia nostra sanctifica: ut quod observantia nostra profitetur extrinsecus, interius operetur. Secret, Saturday of Ember Week in Lent.

[5] Secret, Monday in Holy Week.

[6] Postcommunion, Ember Saturday in Lent.

[7] Secret, Monday in Whitsun Week.

[8] Secret, 9th Sunday after Pentecost.

All that the liturgy says or can say about the value of the Mass is summed up in the words with which Jesus handed over this great sacrifice to His Apostles and ordained them priests forever. "Do this," He said, "in memory of Me" (Luke 22:20). If we offer the sacrifice of the Mass fully conscious that it is the Sacrifice of the Son of God made Man, we will remember first of all its infinite objective value in the sight of God, and we will remember at the same time the love with which Jesus "loved us unto the end."

The Mass is the offering of the Blood of the new "testament." St. Paul likes to play on the word testament, which means not only a covenant, or an agreement, but also a testament in the sense of a last will. The Mass is Christ's supreme gift and legacy to His Church. Here again, we are confronted with a very concrete and objective notion of the character of this One True Sacrifice. The liturgy never ceases to remind us that the Mass is our possession, our inheritance. It is *our sacrifice*. How dear that thought is to the Catholic heart! Morning after morning we are accustomed to hear the priest, turning towards us at the end of the offertory, ask us to "Pray, brethren, that *your sacrifice and mine* may be acceptable" in the eyes of God. Just before the consecration, also, the priest extends his hands over the oblata and prays God to accept "This oblation of our service and of Thy whole family."

We can never forget, therefore, that if Jesus gave Himself for the glory of God on Calvary, He also gave Himself for our salvation at the same time. In His High Priestly prayer, which is apparently the model on which the Canon of the Mass was constructed, Jesus says "For them I sanctify myself (that is to say, I offer myself as a holy sacrifice) that they also may be sanctified in truth, yet not for these only do I pray but for those also who through their word are to believe in me, that all may be one" (John 17:20-21). And the Apostles He ordained that night not only went forth to preach His word, but also ordained other priests who would pass on the priesthood of Christ in their turn to new generations, so that all the ages of the world would share in the sacrifice which Christ had bequeathed, to His beloved Spouse, the Church, as her most precious treasure.

Nowhere more than in the Mass do we see so many aspects of the many-sided charity of the Word made Flesh. First of all there is the love which prompted Him, though equal to the Father, to empty Himself and take the form of a servant, being made man (Phil. 2:7). But He became man not only to live with us, teach us, form us, heal our sicknesses, give us hope. He came also to die for us a most shameful death and with the greatest suffering. He accepts for our sakes every possible injustice and ignominy. But here, too, we see His love for His Father. For in dying to save us, He also satisfied His Father's love for us, and brought about our union with the Father. And finally, He satisfied His own love for His Father. This He did not merely by dying in obedience to His Father's will, as we all know, but above all by accepting death with the full consciousness that He would rise again from death, by the power of God, on the third day. In the mysterious words that break forth from the Savior in the Gospel narrative of the time immediately preceding the Passion, we see this deepest of all Christ's motives in accepting His Cross.

Now my soul is troubled, and what shall I say? Father, save me from this hour? No, this is why I came to this hour. *Father, glorify Thy name* (John 12:27).

Father the hour has come. *Glorify thy son that Thy Son may glorify Thee ... I have glorified thee on earth:* I have accomplished the work that Thou hast given me to do. And now do Thou, Father, *glorify me with thyself, with the glory that I had with Thee before the world existed* (John 17:2-4).

This glorification of the Father in the Son consists first of all in the resurrection of Christ from the dead and His ascension into heaven. But it also consists, and this is essential, in the sharing of the resurrection with all those whom the Father has "chosen" to be the members of His Son. The Father is to be glorified *in us*, through the Mass, which communicates to us the merits of the Cross and the glory of the Resurrection.

I have manifested Thy name to those thou hast given me out of the world. They were thine, and Thou hast given them to me, and they have kept Thy word. ... *And the glory that Thou hast given me I have given to them, that they may be one*, even as we are one. I in them and thou in me; that they may be perfected in unity, and *that the world may know that Thou hast sent me, and that Thou hast loved them even as Thou hast loved me* (John 17:6, 22-24).

The sacrifice of the Eucharist is therefore infinitely glorious, not only because of the fact that it represents the immolation of the Incarnate Son of God, but because it brings the risen Christ, in His glorified and transfigured Flesh to the members of His Mystical Body. It unites them in one, as He Himself is one with the Father. It welds them together in the flame of an infinite charity, the Spirit Who proceeds from the Father and the Son. In so doing it manifests, though in mystery, the glory of the Father. Thus far the mystery is seen only through a glass, darkly; through the veils of faith. But day by day we come closer to the final hour in which it will be revealed to us, and we shall see the full glory of the eternal "sacrifice" that is perpetuated in heaven in the glory of the beatific vision.

But Jesus having offered one sacrifice for sins, has taken His place forever at the right hand of God. . . . By one offering He has perfected forever those who are to be sanctified. Since, then, brethren we are free to enter the holies in virtue of blood of Christ, a new and living way which He inaugurated for us through the veil (that is, His flesh) . . . let us draw near with a true heart and fulness of faith, having our hearts cleansed from an evil conscience and the body washed with clean water (Hebrews 10:12, 14, 19-22).

4. Agápe

All that has so far been said about the Eucharist as sacrifice is insufficient to give us a real appreciation of this mystery. As long as we confine our thoughts within the perspectives and limitations of the virtue of religion, which is a part of justice, we cannot see the real meaning of the Sacrifice and Sacrament of the Eucharist. The Sacrifice of the Mass is, indeed, a supreme act of worship. But it is something more. And if we fail to see this "something more" we will fail also in the perfection of our worship. And so it must be made clear that in order to adore God perfectly in the Sacrifice and

Sacrament of the Eucharist, we must love Him. We must enter by love into an intimate union with Him. We must become aware of the fact that this Sacrifice plunges us into the very life of God Who is Love. We must see that the adoration and homage demanded of us by God cannot be anything that falls short of a complete union of love with Him.

Once again, we must be reminded that our view of the Sacrifice of the Mass must not be distorted and caricatured by too close a contact with pagan and natural ideas of sacrifice.

In all natural ideas of sacrifice, and even in the sacrifices of the Old Law, we find that the function of sacrifice is to bear witness to the greatness and power of God to Whom it is offered. And the sacrifice also aims to propitiate that divine power, and to bring about a moral union between God and the ones offering sacrifice. Sacrifice is a sign that God and man agree: that man recognizes the fact that God can be good to him, and has in truth been good to him. Man shows that he hopes God's benevolence toward him will continue. He promises to live a life worthy of that benevolence.

The Paschal sacrifice of the Jews is however something much more precise and definite than the vague recognition of the divine power. It commemorates a particular historical act by which God manifested not only His Power, but also and above all His will to choose for himself from among men a particular people which was to be *His* People. The Paschal sacrifice therefore commemorates not only the rescue of the Jews from Egypt, but also the creation of the Chosen People, God's People— the nation that was to be ruled directly by Him, cared for, guided, taught, formed, nourished, clothed and defended by Him. Hence, the sacrifices of the Old Law have a special significance. They not only express the desire of men to adore the Lord, the Supreme Being. They bear witness to the fact that the People of God are His People, that they belong to Him and live by His will. They are the expression of a very particular union with God —a union with Him Who IS. They are the sign that Israel is faithful to the Living God, faithful to reality, while idolatrous worship is the worship of what is unreal. In all this, the sacrifices of the Old Law prefigure the perfect sacrifice of the New.

We have said that the test of our notions of sacrifice is to be found in the purity of the idea of God to Whom sacrifice is offered.

In order to understand the Christian sacrifice, we must understand something of the Christian teaching about Who God is.

The God of Christianity is not the god of animism or fetishism, not the spirit that is in a thing, not the objectification of a natural force, not a personification of anything. Nor is He only the God of philosophy—the "Supreme Being," the "Absolute," the "First Mover," the infinite Intelligence Who understands Himself and in Whose knowledge of Himself all other beings are known. The Christian teaching on God is based on a revelation out of the darkness of transcendent mystery—a revelation couched in human terms because it is addressed to men, but manifesting a mystery which human concepts can never delimit or contain. The Christian idea of God is contained in three words of the Apostle St. John: *o Theos agápe estin.* "God is love" (I John 4:8).

In order to give us some idea of Who God is, St. John appeals to the highest and purest activity of the human spirit, the noblest expression of the life of man as an intelligent being. Thus he gives us some starting point from which we can go on to an experiential knowledge of God. "Do you know what it is to love? Do you know what it is to rise above yourself by the selfless dedication of yourself to the good of others, so that you find yourself again beyond and above yourself in the other? Do you know what it means to achieve the fullness of your life by devoting yourself to the good of the whole unity of the brethren with whom you are one? Do you know this pure, spiritual activity which brings about the unity of many individuals, in one mystical person, while at the same time raising them to a new perfection of their own individual personality? Then you can begin to realize something of Who God is."

The word St. John uses for love is not *eros* but *agápe*. It is not the word for a passion that springs from the depths of our own need, and cries out to the other for the fulfillment of our desire. *Agápe* is the love that overflows and gives of its fulness, not the hunger that cries out from the depths of its own emptiness. Human love, by its nature, can never be pure *agápe*. Because we are in ourselves contingent and insufficient, our love necessarily contains an element of *eros*, or passion, springing from our poverty and yearning for the satisfaction of our needs. God, Who needs nothing, can give Himself without limit, and His love—the love which He *is*—is an infinite giving of Himself, eternally replenished from the fullness of His own giving. Hence it is that God is at the same time infinitely rich and infinitely poor, infinitely great and infinitely humble, so far above all that He can place Himself beneath all and no one will see the difference, because, wherever He is, He is both above and below, both this side of us and beyond us, within us and outside us, deeper in us than we are in ourselves, and yet so infinitely far beyond us that we can never reach Him.

For *agápe* to enter into the spirit of man, God must reveal and give His own love, His own life to man. The charity (*agápe*) of the Christian is there-

fore something essentially different from and more
pure than the purest natural disinterested love of
man for his fellow man. It is something altogether
new, a manifestation of God living in mankind, and
revealing His own nature by the love with which
He has decreed to unite men to Himself and to one
another, by incorporating them in His Mystery.

What is the divine *agápe?* What is this charity
which is the very nature of God? Theology describes the Love which is the nature of God when
it exposes to us the dogma of the Three Persons of
God united in One Nature. The sublime mystery
of the Trinity is an elucidation of what is contained in the words of St. John: "God is love." To
say that God is a Father from Whom procedes a
Son Who is united with Him in One Spirit is to
say that God is an infinite "giving" of life, in which
the Three Divine Persons subsist by giving themselves to one another. And it is important, here more
than anywhere else, to avoid human imagery in
the mysteries of God. The Church indulgently permits the representation of the Holy Trinity in pictures, but if we really want to grasp something of
this ineffable mystery the best thing we can do is
to begin by putting all such pictures far from our
minds.

Precisely the great means which the Church has
given us for entering into the Mystery of the Holy
Trinity is the Sacrament and Sacrifice of the Euch-

arist. Instead of trying to imagine the Father, Son and Holy Spirit, we must fix our eyes upon the Sacred Host and remember the words which Jesus spoke at the Last Supper. "He that seeth me seeth the Father also. How sayest thou, show us the Father? Have I been so long a time with you and you have not known me? Do you not believe that I am in the Father and the Father in me?" (John 14:9–10).

We enter into the Mystery of the Holy Trinity not so much by thinking and imagining, as by loving. Thought and imagination soon reach the limits beyond which they cannot pass, and these limits still fall infinitely short of the reality of God. But love, overstepping all bounds and flying beyond· limitations with the wings of God's own Spirit, penetrates into the very depths of the mystery and apprehends Him Whom our intelligence is unable to see. "But to us God has revealed (these things) by His Spirit. For the Spirit searches all things, yea the deep things of God" (I Corinthians 2:10). "Every one that loveth is born of God and knoweth God. . . . No man hath seen God at any time. If we love one another, God abideth in us and His charity is perfected in us. In this we know that we abide in Him and He in us: because He hath given us of His Spirit" (I John 4:7,12,13).

The sacrifice of the Mass is the ritual mystery which reproduces and makes present among us the great action of the Incarnate Word which most clearly and fully manifested on earth, and in time, the timeless and supreme perfection of the divine *agápe*. This action was the mystery of His death on the Cross.

The Love of the Father for the Son burst forth from within the mystery of the Trinity and made itself known outside of God when the Father gave His only begotten Son for mankind. In the Incarnation, the love of the Father for the Son reached out to embrace mankind in the same unity of Spirit in which the Son is one with the Father. Jesus, in turn, dying on the Cross, manifested at the same time His love for the Father and His love for mankind: for it was at the same time the Father's will that He should die for us, and our own best interest, since our salvation depended upon it. In the death of Jesus on the Cross we see the One Love which is God and we see the Three Divine Persons loving one another, and we are ourselves caught up in the bond of love, the circuit of mutual giving, which unites them with One Another.

"God so loved the world as to give His only begotten Son" (John 3:16). "In this we have known the charity of God, because He hath laid down His life for us, and we ought to lay down our lives for the brethren" (I John 3:16). "By this hath the charity of God appeared towards us, because God hath sent His only begotten Son into the world, that we may live by Him. . . . And we have seen and do testify that the Father hath sent His Son to be the Savior of the World" (I John 4:9,14).

The love by which the Son receives all from the Father and gives Himself back to the Father is, in the bosom of God, the eternal "sacrifice" in which the Son acknowledged the Love of the Father. This perfect sacrifice is consummated in the flame of the Holy Spirit, a sacrifice not of death but of life, not of sorrow and destruction but of supreme and productive joy: from this joy springs not only all creation but all the other works by which the divine *agápe* is outwardly manifested. The most perfect of these works is the redemptive death of Christ on the Cross, and this work is perpetuated on our altars by the Sacrifice and Sacrament of the Eucharist.

It is clear, therefore, that in order to appreciate the full meaning of the eucharistic sacrifice, we must remember that the Mass, by making present the great redemptive mystery of the Cross also by that very fact manifests, in mystery, the *agápe* which is the secret and ineffable essence of God Himself. What we behold at Mass is the very reality of God's own love. And we enter into that reality. We are enclosed in the embrace of the Holy Spirit of Truth and Love, the bond which unites the Word and the Father. We become able to unite ourselves with the Word in the great act of sacrificial love by which He bore witness on the Cross to

53

His love for the Father and for us. And at the same time we unite ourselves—in the very heart of the Mystery—with the eternal love by which, as Word, He offers His endless "sacrifice" of praise to the Father in the depths of the Holy Trinity.

III

BEHOLD I AM WITH YOU

1. The Real Presence

It is now time to look more closely at the dogma of the real presence of Jesus Christ in the Blessed Eucharist.

The Council of Trent (Session xiii, canon 1.) clearly defines the truth which is the very foundation of all Christian life and worship. "In the Most Holy Sacrament of the Eucharist there is contained truly, really and substantially, the Body and Blood of Our Lord Jesus Christ, together with His soul and divinity, indeed the whole Christ." The presence of Christ in this sacrament is therefore both *real* and *integral*. It is a real presence because the Blessed Sacrament is not merely a sign or symbol of Christ as the "Bread of Life." Nor is it simply a figure which arouses our faith and devotion and stirs up our hearts to greater charity towards God and our neighbors. Nor does Christ simply act on us through the Sacrament. He is present in the consecrated species not merely by His activity but in His substance, and it is this which makes the Eucharist different from all the other sacraments and elevates it so far above them all. The Blessed Sacrament not only imparts grace as an instrument of Christ the Sanctifier but it contains Him Who is the source and author of all sanctity: *ipsum sanctitatis fontem et auctorem continet.*[1]

This is the only way in which the Church has ever interpreted the clear statement of Jesus Christ when He Himself blessed bread, broke it, gave it to His disciples saying: "This is My Body." Not until many centuries had gone by was the reality of Christ's presence in the Eucharist called into question by anyone who claimed to be a Christian.

Moreover, the consecrated species of bread contains Christ's Body as a direct effect of the words of consecration. But not only the Body of Christ is there. Everything that belongs to the integrity of His Person is present also with His sacred Body, by concomitance. In enumerating the Body and Blood, soul, divinity of the Lord, the Council of Trent was not reducing Christ to a collection of fragments, still less of abstractions, but only fulfilling its mani-

---

[1] *Catechismus Concilii Tridentini*, II, 4, 1.

fest duty to make clear the belief of the Church in the wholeness of Christ's real presence. What we have in the Eucharist is not simply a mental object made up of six or seven concepts fused into one. We have a Person, and much more than anything than we can conceive by the word "person." Even in the human sense, every living person is by his very spirituality and concreteness, an existential mystery which we cannot penetrate by analysis. Here we have not only the mystery of a human soul in all its unique spiritual intimacy, not merely the human person in the ineffable concreteness of life and spiritual self-determination; but a human nature united to the Word of God, subsisting in a divine Person. The mystery of the Incarnation is deep enough, in itself: but when Christ dwelt among us as a historical Person, at least His humanity was evident, even though His divinity remained hidden. But here in this admirable Sacrament both humanity and divinity are hidden. Yet the Sacrament is none the less Christ, the whole Christ, really and integrally present as a Person.

Everything that belongs to the reality of a man's body is here. Everything that is proper to His soul, everything that makes Him a Person, all that He is as Christ, the Son of Man, the Son of God: everything is present here. As the Church teaches us, we have here in this Sacrament the same Christ Who was born of the Virgin Mary and Who is now enthroned in glory at the right hand of the Father.[2]

When all this has been said, we are only at the threshold of the mystery of the Eucharist as Sacrament. In the sacraments we have an entirely unique order of being, and to appreciate the mystery of the Holy Eucharist we have to bear this fact in mind. The Blessed Eucharist is not a wafer of unleavened bread which somehow contains the substance of the Body of Christ. It is no longer bread. It no longer has the being, or the nature of any material object. The sensible accidents of bread remain, it is true, but they do not inhere in any substance. The Being Who is present is entirely invisible, because Christ in this Sacrament is present only in the manner of a substance. The substance of a thing is its aptitude to be what it is, its aptitude to exist by itself, its power to be itself. It is the substance that answers our question "what is this?" Now in the Sacrament of the Eucharist, precisely, when we ask this question of the consecrated Host, we must listen to the answer of faith, which responds in the words of Christ "This is My Body." The words "My Body" designate the only substantial being which is now present. There no longer remains anything of the substance of bread. We see the accidents of bread, but they contain the substance of the Body of

---

[2]Verum Christi Domini corpus, illud, quod natum ex virgine in coelis sedet ad dexteram Patris, hoc Sacramento contineri. *Catechismus Concilii Tridentini,* II, 4, 26.

Christ. Hence we can readily understand the words of a profound modern theologian of the Eucharist, Dom Anscar Vonier, when he says:

The sacraments have a mode of existence of their own, a psychology of their own, a grace of their own. If they are not beings in the sense in which a man is a being, or an angel is a being, they are beings nevertheless resembling God's nature very closely. It is no doubt a constant tendency in us to make of the sacraments things easily classified under the ordinary headings of human concepts; yet let us remember that sacramental thought is something quite *sui generis* and the less anthropomorphism, or even the less spiritism be introduced into it, the better for our theology.[3]

He adds that the world of the sacraments will not reveal itself to us without a stern effort on our part to cultivate truly sacramental thought, but such an effort is certainly most rewarding. It will make us, as he says, "true mystics."[4]

---

[3] *The Key to the Doctrine of the Eucharist,* London, 1925, p. 36.
[4] Id., p. 41.

2. Sacramental Contemplation

True contemplation of the mystery of the Eucharist is not possible, in the last analysis, if we do not resist the temptations to anthropomorphism or to spiritism which beset us when we try to explain to ourselves the real presence and its consequences. Anthropomorphism in this case consists usually in confusing the concept of Christ's natural, local or physical presence (by which He is present in heaven) with His sacramental presence in the Blessed Eucharist. Spiritism is a more subtle temptation which either ignores or overlooks the sacramental species altogether, or else regards Christ's presence in the Sacrament as identical with the presence of a soul in a body.

It is true that the Body of Christ, being present in this Sacrament after the manner of a substance, is entirely present in every part of the Host, and in the whole Host at the same time, and this is analogous to the presence of a soul in a body. But Christ is not present to the Host as a new substantial form. Also, it is most important to remember that a sacrament is not a purely spiritual thing: it is sensible, and therefore its material element is essential to its reality.

The more exact our considerations remain, the more easily will we be able to avoid misunderstandings of the real Presence. Let us return to the Council of Trent. Having told us that the Body of Christ is really present in the Blessed Sacrament, and that this Body of Christ is the same which is enthroned in heaven, the Church explains to us that there is here no contradiction.

There is no conflict in the fact that Our Savior Himself is always seated at the right hand of the Father *in His natural mode of being* and that at the same time He is none the less present in many places *sacramentally* in His substance in a manner of being which, though we can hardly express it in words, is nevertheless possible to God.[5]

Here we must emphasize the distinction made by the Church between Christ's natural presence and His presence in the Sacrament. Both presences are real, and both are *equally real*, but nevertheless only the former is strictly a "local" presence. For only in His own quantitative dimensions is the Body of Christ directly localized—and this direct localization is realized in heaven, but not on our altars, where He is present indirectly localized by the quantitative dimensions of the Host. These dimen-

---

[5] Session xiii, chapter 1.

sions are not His own, and He is therefore not in immediate physical contact with His material surroundings. His contact with us is spiritual and mystical.

The presence of Christ in the Blessed Sacrament is therefore not a local presence. He becomes present in the Host not by any change in Himself but by a change which He effects, by divine power, in the bread, converting its substance into His own Body. Transubstantiation is no sense a "production" of the Body of Christ, or a local "adduction" of His Flesh. This is not so hard to conceive if we remember that He did exactly the same thing at the Last Supper. Nothing happened to His own Person when He pronounced the words which changed bread into His Body. He remained locally present at the head of the supper table and became sacramentally present in the Bread which He had changed, by transubstantiation, into Himself, and which was eaten by the disciples.

However, an important distinction is called for here. Since the accidents of bread which "contain" the substance of Christ's Body are themselves localized, they determine His sacramental presence within the limits of the space which they themselves occupy. That is how we say that the Body of Christ is "in the tabernacle" or "in the monstrance" or "on the Paten." He is substantially where the bread was. Again, we must repeat that the sacramental presence of Christ is no less real than His natural presence. He is just as truly present in the Blessed Sacrament as He is in heaven, but the mode of His presence is entirely different, and this fact is often forgotten by pious writers, who treat the sacramental presence as if it were only a thinly disguised local presence. Actually it is a completely different kind of presence, unique and without any parallel in the natural order.

In Aristotelian metaphysics a material substance enters into contact with external reality only through the accidents which complete it. Now the proper accidents of the body of Christ are hidden, as it were, within His substance. Consequently He is not in direct physical contact with any material or spatial reality, and he cannot perform any bodily action or undergo any suffering which implies that kind of contact. When the Host is divided at the *Pax Domini*, the Body of Christ is not divided, still less does it suffer. If the Host is corrupted in the tabernacle, the Body of Christ is not corrupted. When the accidents of bread and wine are dissolved within the communicant, the Body of Christ is not dissolved. But when He is received in Communion, He is received in all literal truth because the *substance* of His Body and Blood is given us in Communion.

At the same time, we must remember that Christian devotion never in practice separates the accidents of bread from the substance of Christ under the sacramental species. The Sacrament is an integral unity, and it is also a sensible thing. The adoration that is offered to the Blessed Eucharist is offered to Jesus Christ Who is really present in the sacrament, and the fact that His Body does not suffer when the accidents of Bread are broken would be no reason for treating the sacramental species with carelessness or indifference. They are to be respected for the sake of Him whom they contain and Whom we adore in them. If all the creatures of God are good and holy because they have felt the touch of His creative hand, how much more holy are those humble material elements which the divine power has elevated to so sublime a function as that of playing an instrumental part in His work of sanctification? And above all, what reverence ought we to have for the plain, humble species which He has deigned to take as His sacred vesture in coming to us as the food of our souls?

At the same time, we must carry this sense of the unity of the sacramental being still further. The Eucharist is not a symbol of something greater than itself. It is not merely a "sign" of the Body of Christ, it *is* the Body of Christ. This cannot be repeated too often.

Hence we do not have to strain our minds or our imaginations to see *through* the Sacrament. Euch-

aristic contemplation is not a game of hide and seek
in which, if we find the secret formula of prayer,
we can unveil the hidden Christ. This mistake is
harmful for our own souls and pays no real honor
to the Blessed Sacrament. Indeed it implies a funda-
mental misconception of what the Sacrament is. It
presupposes that the Sacrament is a being which
conceals another being: and this other reality is the
natural presence of Christ. By no means! As St.
Thomas says: "Our bodily eye is prevented from
a direct vision of Christ's Body through those sacramental species under which it exists, not only as
through a kind of cover, as we cannot see what is
hidden through some bodily veil, but because
Christ's body bears a relation to the medium which
surrounds this Sacrament, not through its own accidents, but through the sacramental species."[6]

And Dom Vonier adds that the sacraments of the
New Law are by no means the "weak and lowly
elements" which St. Paul scorned, that is to say
veils of higher realities. "They are not veiling anything, but they are complete realities in themselves,
existing in their own right. . . . There is nothing
like the sacraments in heaven or on the earth, and it
would be a great disparagement of their character
to look upon them as mere veils of more substantial
spiritual realities."[7]

---

[6] *Summa Theologica* III, Q.76, art.7, ad 1.
[7] *Op. cit.*, p. 36.

He adds that sacraments are not substitutes for anything else, and the sacramental presence of Christ is not a cloak for His natural presence. Indeed he points out that if Christ were naturally present on the altar at the moment of consecration the Sacrament would lose its meaning, its truth and its reason for existing. Christ is present under the appearance of Bread and not in His own natural presence, precisely in order to safeguard the truth and mystery of the Sacrament. His presence must be such that it is *essentially invisible*, that it transcends all the powers of our interior and exterior senses, and is accessible *only to our faith*. "One is justified in saying that it is the very condition of the sacramental presence to transcend all vision and all experience even of the highest order, because there is really no kind of perceptive power in man, or even in the angel, corresponding to that state of being which is properly the sacramental state."[8]

Vonier here seems to agree with those Thomist theologians who hold that even a miracle would never enable us to perceive the true Body of Christ in this Sacrament with our bodily eyes, simply because there is no way in which a substance can be seen with the eyes. We must see Him with the eyes of our spirit, illuminated by loving faith.

---

[8] Vonier, *op. cit.*, p. 33.

3. The Soul of Christ in the Eucharist

We have said that the Body of Christ is present by the power of the words of consecration, and His soul and divinity by concomitance. This distinction, though important, should not lead us to introduce a division into the Person of Christ sacramentally present in the Eucharist. His soul and divinity are not simply in the background in a latent, inert and more or less abstract fashion. In this sacrament of His love, Christ is present with all His powers and all His capacities disposed to act and operate with all the actions and "passions" (in the metaphysical sense) which belong to His glorified life in heaven. There is only one exception to be made. Since His body is not in touch with material reality by contact of quantitative dimensions, He does not exercise His sense faculties in this Sacrament, at least not in any natural way. He does not see us with His bodily eyes, but after all He has no need to do so since His divine vision illumines His human mind with a far deeper and more intimate knowledge of us than we can possibly conceive.

Christ in the tabernacle sees and knows us far more clearly than we see and know ourselves. The knowledge of us that exists within the sacramental Christ Whom we receive in Communion is a knowledge He has already gained from the depths of our own being. Therefore Jesus in the Blessed Sacrament does not scrutinize us coldly as objects, as beings remote from Himself and still retaining some traces of the enigmatic. He knows us in Himself, as His "other selves." He knows us subjectively, as though we were an extension of His own Person—which indeed we are. This knowledge by identity is the knowledge not only of science but of love. Modern psychology has coined the word "empathy"—the knowledge of a person by another from "within" by a projected sympathy which lives through the experiences of the one known as they appear to him. But this human empathy is still a remote and uncertain thing, which cannot completely bridge the gap between two separate spirits. The "empathy" with which we are understood by Christ proceeds from the depths of our own being, and is so deep that if we would find out the truth about ourselves we must seek it in Him, at the moment of Holy Communion. For Christ is our own deepest and most intimate "self," our higher self, our new self as sons of God. That is what it means for us to say, with St. Paul, "for me to live is Christ" (Philippians 1:21). The peace which opens out in the depths of our soul, the spiritual silence, the rest, the security, the certainty that come to us at Communion with the intimate awareness of His presence, is a sign that we have opened the door that leads into the inner sanctuary of our own being, the secret place where we are united with God. This is the "chamber" which we should enter when we go to pray to our Father in secret (Matthew 6:6). In reality, it can only be opened to us by Him who taught us that it is the place where we must retire to pray.

To human eyes, Christ in the Blessed Sacrament would seem altogether inert and passive. Nevertheless it is He who calls us to Communion by the action of interior and secret inspirations, because He knows that we need this mystical food. And when we receive the sacred Host, it is not only because we ourselves have a desire to receive Him, but also and above all because Christ, in this Sacrament, desires to give Himself to us. In the words of St. Ambrose: "Hast thou come to the altar? It is the Lord Jesus that calls thee . . . saying 'Let him kiss me with the kiss of his mouth' . . . He sees thee to be free of sins, because they have been cleansed away. Therefore He judges thee worthy of the heavenly sacraments and therefore He invites thee to the heavenly banquet."[9]

---

[9] St. Ambrose, *De Sacramentis*, V, 2-5, 6.

The charity of Christ which motivates His will, hidden in the Blessed Eucharist, is the same infinite love for all men which draws them to union with the Father in Himself, by the grace of the Holy Spirit. Again, this love is not merely a universal charity which embraces all without exception, but it also reaches out to each one in the inscrutable hiddenness of his own unique individuality. Just as Christ on the Cross "loved *me* and delivered Himself up for *me* (Galatians 2:20), so here too he loves *me* and comes to *me* in the Blessed Sacrament. When He finds Himself united to me in Communion, He is by no means surprised to learn that I am a sinner. He knew that before, and He loved me as I am. He comes to me because He is still the friend and the refuge and the Savior of sinners. For my part I should do my best to respond to His love, even though I may be unworthy of it. And the best way to respond is to believe in its inexpressible reality and act according to my belief.

The action of the Blessed Sacrament upon my soul at the moment of Communion is, as we shall see, the action of the divine and spiritual energy which resides in the Body of Christ. This spiritual energy is first of all divine light, and then it is perfect charity. It radiates from the Body of Christ which we receive in Communion, and it penetrates our whole being, transforming and divinizing us by His power. But the action of this supernatural energy which radiates from the transfigured and glorified Body of the Savior is not exercised without the movement of His own will. The grace that we receive by contact with Him is a grace which He wills us to receive, and it is poured out with a generosity proportionate to His personal love for us and to His intimate knowledge of our personal needs. Nowhere is it more true to say that the graces we receive are strictly according to the measure of the giving of Christ (*secundum mensuram donationis Christi*, Ephesians 4:7).

The Love of Christ in this Sacrament enlarges our capacity to receive grace and moves us to acts of a more fervent and more spiritual charity. It is by a movement of the will of Christ that we receive the grace of the Holy Spirit Who, as Scheeben says, is the spiritual fire which bursts forth from the immolated Lamb in the Eucharist. Here are some of the texts in which this great nineteenth century theologian brings us the very heart of the doctrine of the Fathers:

In its own glorified state the Body of Christ is, so to speak, the wheat living by the power of the Holy Spirit; in the Eucharist it is the bread baked by the fire of the Holy Spirit, whereby the Holy Spirit confers life on others ... The Flesh of Christ imparts life ... by the Spirit, the divine energy residing in it. "The Flesh of the Lord is life-giving spirit" says St. Athanasius, "because it was conceived of the life-giving Spirit.

71

What is born of the Spirit is spirit. . . ." Now the Lamb of God, slain from the beginning of the world before the eyes of God, has to stand before God as an eternal holocaust, burning with the fire of the Spirit.[10]

The human will of Christ, the Savior of the world, perfectly united forever with the will of God the Father in this sacrifice, elicits each movement by which the Holy Spirit proceeds into our hearts and draws us to union with the Logos. The Spirit, in turn, awakens in our hearts a deep mystical response to the action of the Incarnate Word Who has come to us in communion. The Spirit reveals to us the reality of Christ's presence and the immensity of His love for us. The Spirit opens the secret, inner ear of our own spirit so that we are able to distinguish the pure tones of the voice of Christ, the Man-God, speaking within our own souls which He has so intimately united to His own soul. Finally, by our response to this movement of the Spirit of God, sent into our hearts by the action of Christ's personal love for us, we unite our wills perfectly with the will of Christ, our minds with His mind, our hearts with His Sacred Heart and become "one spirit" with Him, according to the saying of St. Paul: "He who is joined to the Lord is one spirit" (I Corinthians 6:17). Then the

[10] Scheeben, *The Mysteries of Christianity*, pp. 515, 517, 518, 519.

Father, looking upon us, sees no one but Christ, His beloved Son, in Whom He is well pleased.

We have seen that it is by an act of His own will that Christ becomes present, in the miracle of transubstantiation, in the consecrated Host. Scheeben tells us that there is only one reason why Christ wills to make Himself present in the Eucharist: "That He may unite Himself with individual men in communion and become one body with them . . . that He may become man in each man, by taking the human nature of each into union with His own."[11] It is therefore clear that in this sacrament Christ comes to us with a most ardent and personal love for each one of us and that our reception of the sacrament means nothing at all if it does not imply a recognition of this love and a sincere desire to give ourselves to Him as He gives Himself to us, by a union of our will with His in pure charity.

Not only are the divinely illumined intelligence and will of Christ living and active in this Sacrament, but also His memory. And here too we find ourselves in the presence of an action that transcends anything that we can imagine from our own experience. Remember that the Mass makes present to us the sacrifice of Calvary. Jesus needs no sacramental mystery to make Calvary present to Himself. The Mass is not for Him as it is for us a "me-

---

[11] *Op. cit.*, p. 486.

morial" of the Passion, for by virtue of the hypostatic union He sees now, as He did then, all things and all ages as present to God's eternity. Consequently, although He now reigns glorious and impassible in heaven, nevertheless the Passion is present to Him. But also, and this is even more worthy to be remembered by us, the Mass brings to us *Christ in His Passion*. That is to say that we who assist at Mass, and who receive Him in Communion are present to Him in His Passion. The depths of our souls, with all our sins, weaknesses, sufferings, limitations and trials lie wide open to the eyes of the Savior's spirit in Gethsemani and on the Cross. What we are now, our dispositions, our frailties, our good and evil desires, were all vividly present to His mind then. It is on the basis of this shattering truth that Pope Pius XI could say that our efforts to love Christ now, and especially our desire to console the Redeemer by communions of reparation, can be believed to have actually consoled Him in His Passion two thousand years ago. "For if on account of our sins which were then future but foreseen, the soul of Christ (in the agony) became sorrowful unto death, there is no doubt that He also even then received no little solace from our acts of reparation, also foreseen when the angel of heaven appeared to Him to console His Heart oppressed by anguish and sorrow." (*Miserentissimus Redemptor,* May 8, 1928.)

This brings us to a distinction which has to be made, if we are to understand the Blessed Eucharist properly. Failure to make this distinction involves theologians and preachers and men of prayer in confusing difficulties. What is worse, it sometimes leads them into futile discussions and misunderstandings with one another. For some of them seem to think that the Christ of the Eucharist is only the glorified Christ reigning in heaven, and others speak as if He were only the Christ of Calvary. Actually, He is both at the same time.

The substance of the Body of Christ made present by the words of Consecration is the living, actual substance of the Body in which Christ is naturally present in heaven. It is therefore the substance of a glorified Body. It is not a dead, crucified Body, not even a suffering Body endowed with mortal life. The Christ of the Eucharist is immortal. This is the Body of the King of Glory.

However, we must remember that there is a twofold consecration in the Mass. The species of Bread and Wine are separately consecrated, so that the Body of Christ is present on the altar mystically separated from His Blood. It is by virtue of this separation that Christ is immolated and offered to the Father in a state of victimhood. Hence the glorified Body of Christ, without any suffering, without any physical change whatever in His own being, is mystically placed in the same condition in which He expiated the sins of the world on the Cross. In the Mass therefore it is Christ Crucified who is present on the altar. It is the Christ Who suffered for us, *Christum passum*, that we offer to the Father, not the glorious Christ, even though it is the glorified Body of Christ that is placed here in a state of immolation. What is the distinction? Christ the King and High Priest, reigning in glory, acting through the person of His consecrated minister, makes present His glorified Flesh and Blood under the sacramental veils. The Body that is present is the true, living Body of Christ in glory. This is the real presence, effected by transubstantiation.

But in addition to this real sacramental presence affected by the words of consecration, there is also the presence of Christ crucified, effected by the symbolic separation of the Body and Blood of the Lord. Present in His glorified Body by transubstantiation, He is present as "crucified" in a representative rite. And it is this second presence that we might call more properly a presence "in mystery," using the word mystery not merely in the sense of something incomprehensible, but in the ancient sense of a divine action manifesting the intervention of the eternal God in the world of space and time in order to unite men to Himself.

Theologians argue whether this presence of Christ in Mystery is the presence of Christ Who has suffered (*Christus Passus*) or even more strictly of the Passion of Christ (*Passio Christi*). And among those that hold that the very Passion itself is present, some declare that it is present as a "real efficacy rather than as an efficacious reality," while Dom Odo Casel declares that in the Mass the Passion of Christ is made present in a real, supratemporal, and objective sense and that the ritual mystery makes the work of our Redemption present not only in its effects but in its substance.[12] The sacrifice of the Eucharist is not another act of Christ, repeating His immolation on the Cross, nor even a repetition of the same act: it is the very act itself, anticipated at the Last Supper and perpetuated on our altars, and even, Casel would add, in the administration of the other sacraments.

Whatever may be the eventual conclusion of the Church in this dispute of theologians, all must agree with Pope Pius XII who says in *Mediator Dei* that in the Mass the "sacrifice of the Redeemer is shown forth in an admirable manner by external signs which are symbols of His death," that the "Most Holy Eucharist is the culmination and center of the Christian religion" and that all should realize that it is their chief duty and dignity to be able to participate, through the Mystery of the Eucharist in the redeeming sacrifice of Christ on the Cross.

Although the Holy See has decreed in modern

---

12 Cf. Dom Eloi Dekkers, *La Maison Dieu,* 14.

times that before the altar breads are baked for Mass they should be stamped with an image of the crucified, it is evident that no such representation is needed for the devotion of a priest who has an elementary sense of the meaning of the sacred rites. There is no clearer, no simpler, no more eloquent or more literal act of symbolism in all the liturgy than the sacramental separation of the Body and Blood of Christ on the altar at Mass. The severity of the liturgy is here transfigured by its own simplicity, so that we see before us on the altar the sublime sobriety of Christ Himself. The eloquence of this tremendous, yet silent rite is the perfect eloquence with which God Himself, in the simplest of human words and with the most common and ordinary of human things, instituted the sacrament which opens to us the gate of heaven. *O salutaris hostia, quae caeli pandis ostium!*

Hence although the Christ of the Eucharist is in all truth the whole Christ, the living, glorified Christ with all that He has and all that He is, body and soul, man and God, yet in the most proper special meaning of the Eucharist we have here before us Christ crucified, Christ the Redeemer. His very presence speaks to us in the words of St. Paul, admonishing us to: "Be therefore imitators of God as most dear children, and walk in love as Christ also has loved us, and delivered Himself up for us an offering and a sacrifice to God to ascend as an odor of sweetness" (Ephesians 5:1).

It is clear that if the Body and Blood of Christ are made present to us here in a state of immolation, His soul is also present in a most special way with those dispositions with which He was immolated for us. Here at the Mass we are confronted with the same Christ "who though he was by nature God did not consider being equal to God a thing to be clung to but emptied Himself, taking the nature of a slave and being made like unto men. And appearing in the form of a man He humbled Himself, becoming obedient unto death, even to death on a Cross" (Philippians 2:5–8).

If we are to unite ourselves with His sacrifice in the most perfect manner we must strive as far as possible to unite ourselves with these dispositions of His soul. This is one of the main themes of *Mediator Dei.*

Quoting St. Augustine, Pius XII says that in the Sacrament of the altar "the Church sees that in what she offers she herself is offered."[13] But in order for the sacraments and the Mass to achieve their full effects in the hearts of the faithful, each one must make personal and interior efforts to dispose his own heart and bring it into union with the Heart of Christ. "In order that the oblation by

---

[13] *The City of God*, X, 6.

which the faithful offer the divine victim in this sacrifice ... may have its full effect, it is necessary that the faithful add ... the offering of themselves as victims" (*Mediator Dei*). What does this mean? It means first of all that "each one's faith must be more ready to work through charity," that each one's piety may become more fervent and more real and finally that each may not only share Christ's consuming desire for His Father's glory, but also come to resemble Him as closely as possible in the patience, meekness, obedience, humility and love with which He bore His most grievous sufferings.

These efforts of each individual Christian to reproduce the virtues and dispositions of Christ do not end in the moral perfection of the individual alone. We must always remember that we are not sanctified as isolated units but as members of a living organism, the Church: we are sanctified as "members one of another." The growth of each individual person in Christlike virtue contributes all the more to the Christ-likeness of the whole Church, and perfects her union with her divine Bridegroom. It is therefore not only a question of individuals *imitating* the divine Redeemer and thus perfecting their own lives, but above all of Christ living more and more perfectly in His Church by virtue of the fact that His Spirit takes fuller and deeper possession of all its individual members uniting them more perfectly to one another and to Himself.

Therefore all the virtues of Christ crucified should be reproduced in the faithful with a particular orientation: they should be directed to the union of the faithful in Christ. The patience of the Redeemer must be reproduced in our lives not merely by the fact that we bear with one another, but that we forgive one another *in order to be more closely united in Christ.* His charity should burn in our hearts not merely in order that we ourselves may be more perfect, but also in order that we may more perfectly share with our brothers and even with our enemies, the peace and joy of the risen Christ. Our humility is to be directed not only to ornamenting our own soul with the spiritual beauty which this virtue produces in us, but above all it is aimed at keeping us firmly united with our brothers and our superiors in the bond of peace. The same applies to our obedience, our longsuffering, our meekness, our almsdeeds, our mercy, and all the rest. Everything is ordered to the building up of the Body of Christ.

The dispositions with which the soul of Christ is present on the altar in the Blessed Sacrament can easily be learned from the passages in which the Epistle to the Hebrews describes Him as High Priest and Victim of the one true sacrifice. He is faithful above all to God (Hebrews 3:2). But He is also faithful to His chosen ones, His "own house," and "We are that house if we hold fast our confidence" (3:6). He has "entered into His rest" (4:10) but He sees us all for "there is no creature hidden from His sight: but all things are naked and open to the eyes of Him to whom we have to give an account" (4:13). He does not gaze on us with the cold, critical eye of a severe judge; "For we have not a high priest who cannot have compassion on our infirmities, but one tried as we are in all things except sin" (4:15). He is humble in His priesthood (5:5) which is perfect and eternal, and "enables Him at all times to save those who come to God through Him" (7:25). Above all, "He lives always to make intercession for us" (idem.). Of course, He is "holy, innocent and undefiled, set apart from sinners and become higher than the heavens" (7:26). This is necessary "for if He were on earth He would not even be a priest" (8:4). In offering for us His Blood, in heaven, He still retains forever the dispositions which the Psalmist foretold of Him, and which made obsolete the fruitless sacrifices of the Old Law: they are the dispositions with which He offered Himself on Calvary: "Sacrifice and oblation thou wouldst not, but a body thou hast fitted to me: in holocausts and sin offerings thou hast had no pleasure. Then said I: behold I come, in the head of the book it is written of me that I may do

Thy will O God" (Psalms 39:7 f). This perfect obedience to the will of God is the very heart of Christ's sacrifice and ours. "It is in this will that we have been sanctified through the offering of the Body of Jesus once for all" (10:10). Hence it is that there is no longer any need for bloody sacrifices on earth, or for any other sacrifice than that which has been offered once for all by Christ, for "where there is forgiveness for sin, there is no longer offering for sin" (10:18). Finally, these most beautiful verses of all:

For Jesus in the days of His earthly life, with a loud cry and tears offered up prayers and supplications to Him who was able to save Him from death and was heard because of His reverent submission. And He, Son though He was, learned obedience from the things which He suffered; and when perfected He became to all who obey Him the cause of eternal salvation (Hebrews 5:7-9).

Here in a few words we have the portrait of the Redeemer Who makes Himself present in His one perfect Sacrifice on the altar at Mass. We have also the model to Whom we must conform ourselves as we unite ourselves to Him. For as we approach the altar we are reminded by the very acts which we perform that we must obey Christ as He has obeyed His Father, for as the Father has sent Him into the world, so Jesus has sent us (John 17:18).

So much for the special significance of the Eucharist as a memorial of the Passion of Christ. But there is much more even than this. For in common with all the other sacraments, the Blessed Eucharist also has a threefold signification which not only touches the present and reaches into the past, but also goes forward into the future. In the words of St. Thomas:

Properly speaking a sacrament is a sign of our sanctification, in which we may consider three aspects: that is first of all the Passion of Christ, which is the cause of our sanctification; then the form of our sanctification, which consists in grace and the virtues, and the last end of our sanctification which is eternal life.[14]

Hence in the Sacrament of the Eucharist we have the Body of Christ present first of all as the cause of our sanctification, since it is in a state of mystical immolation which makes present the Redeeming Sacrifice of Calvary. Then we have the Body of Christ as the "form" of present grace, which is the effect of the Passion. Of this we shall see more later. Finally we have the Body of Christ present as the source of our beatitude in heaven. For the same Body hidden in the Sacrament is the fountain of light and glory which, by the action of His will and of His love for us, will communicate to us the vision of God.

---

14 *Summa Theologica*, III Q.60, a.3.

So we find that in this ineffable mystery of God's love we can have in all literal truth a foretaste of our happiness in heaven, for we receive in Communion Him Who is the very source and substance of our blessedness in God. As we kneel after Mass to make our thanksgiving, how can we avoid hearing in our hearts some faint sound of the voice which will one day say to us, if we are faithful to Him, "Come you blessed of my Father, enter into the joy which was prepared for you from the beginning of the world" (Matthew 25:34). The possession of heaven is the possession of the glory of Christ. In Communion (and indeed this is one of the most notable as well as one of the least appreciated effects of Communion) Christ gives Himself to us in His glorified Body and soul and in His divinity to be our happiness. We do not yet possess Him in clear vision, but only by the virtue of hope. Hence the importance of coming to Communion with hearts purified not only from sins and attachments, but also from ideas of happiness that are too base and too material and which therefore interfere with the perfection of our union with Him.

It is also very important that in order to purify our hearts and enter more perfectly into the joy of Communion with the Risen Christ, we should strive to free ourselves from the narrow limitations of an individualistic piety which treats Communion as a refuge from the troubles and sorrows of communal

85

living and ends by cutting us off, spiritually, from the Mystical Christ. There is an unconscious and unrecognized infantilism which moves some pious souls to treat Communion uniquely as a source of personal consolation—their meeting with the eucharistic Christ is regarded solely as an occasion to plunge into the darkness and sweetness of their own subjectivity, and rest in the forgetfulness of all else.

It is quite true that Communion lifts us above the cares and confusions of everyday life, and it is also true that the eucharistic Christ comes to us bringing a peace and a quiet illumination of the spirit which elevate the mind beyond the level of concepts and images, and leave it resting, as it were, in the luminous darkness of spiritual understanding. But this mystical "sleep" of the truly enlightened mind is in reality the vigilance of a mature and perfect soul that has found Christ and found, at the same time, all multiplicity reduced to unity in Him. This is, in fact, the apprehension of the sublime objective reality that makes us all one in Christ. But to make Communion a refuge from reality, from social responsibility, from the pain of being a mature person, is in fact to withdraw from Christ into the darkness and inertia of our own subjectivity.

Communion is not a flight from life, not an evasion of reality, but the full acceptance of the responsibilities of our membership in Christ and the total commitment of ourselves to the lives and aims of the Mystical Body of Christ.

The supreme consolation of eucharistic Communion is the hope that possesses in mystery the full glory of Christ that will one day be revealed in His Church. Since the Eucharist signifies not only the true Body of Christ but also His Mystical Body, there are therefore also three presences of the Mystical Body at Mass: first it participates in His Passion, second it shares in the grace which He pours out upon it to sanctify it, and finally, the whole Mystical Body is present at Mass in anticipated glory, by virtue of the hope which animates the whole Church and moves her to cry out, as she does at the end of the Apocalypse, "Come Lord Jesus."

And I saw a new heaven and a new earth. For the first heaven and the first earth passed away, and the sea is no more. And I saw the Holy City, the New Jerusalem, coming down out of heaven from God, made ready as a bride adorned for her husband. And I heard a loud voice from the throne, saying: 'behold the dwelling of God with men, and He will dwell with them. And they will be His people, and God Himself will be with them, as their God. And God will wipe away every tear from their eyes. And death shall be no more: neither shall there be mourning, nor crying nor pain anymore, for the former things have passed away. . . .' (Apocalypse 21:1–4.)

IV

I AM THE WAY

1. Our Journey to God

Every sacramental action performed by the Incarnate Word in and with His Church is a direct, supernatural intervention of God in the affairs of man and of time. The word "intervention" is not strong enough to express how the movements and orientations of human wills are lifted bodily out of their own sphere by an action that is of an altogether different kind, with a completely different direction. The Logos does not merely insert His action into the movement of time, diverting it in a new sense. He does much more than bring to bear an external influence upon something that is already in the process of attaining its end. Nor does He merely "cut across" the stream of history by a diversion that has unexpected implications. The

Scriptures which reveal to us the characteristic modes of God's supernatural action in the world, for the salvation of men, always express them in figurative language, because strictly speaking these interventions of God are mysteries which elude the grasp of human concepts. Yet although these mysteries are beyond all of our ideas and reasoning about them, they are nevertheless very close to us, very accessible, concrete and tangible in all their spiritual reality. Indeed, they enter into the very substance of our ordinary life. Although the most sublime theology cannot fully explain the mystery by which God gives Himself to man in the Eucharist, the reality of our union with Him is something that can be experienced and to some extent appreciated in its spiritual purity by the mind of the simplest child. As St. Thomas explains, applying an Old Testament text in the office of Corpus Christi: "What people is there that has gods as close to it as our God!"

Faith is the door to this experience of spiritual realities: faith which starts with concepts but transcends them, and reaches into the luminous darkness which is not merely "beyond" concepts but also, so to speak, on this side of conceptual knowledge: it is the ineffable darkness of the reality which is too familiar, too intimate to be analyzed. We experience the things of God in much the same way as we experience our own intimate reality, we discover Him in much the same way as we discover the unsuspected depths of our own deep self. The sacraments, springing into being, moving and acting among us with a movement and an action that are half way between the created and the divine, lightly touch our several senses with their simple meanings, and thereby release in the depths of our souls the secret fire of God. Then the sacramental signs disappear, and leave us in the possession of realities that cannot be fully explained in human language. More than that, they leave us profoundly modified by the contact of these realities. Like the pillar of fire that guided the Israelites out of Egypt in the darkness of the night, like the pillar of cloud that led their way by day, sacramental graces draw us out of this world into the desert through which we must travel to reach the Promised Land. By His sacraments, God brings us through the Red Sea that divides the world of flesh from the world of spirit. By His sacraments He leads us through the spiritual wilderness in which we must be purified and formed into His chosen People. In His sacraments He already gives us a foretaste of the peace that will be ours when we reach the Land flowing with milk and honey, the land of spiritual delight and contemplation in which, liberated from the weak and needy elements of this life, we live entirely in the spirit, and are one with God in Christ.

Yet we must never forget the paradox that we are taken "out of this world" while remaining in the world. Our journey into the desert is not a journey in space, but a journey in spirit. Jesus does not pray that we may be taken out of the world physically (John 17:15) but that we may remain in the world and be kept from evil. Remaining in the world, we are nevertheless not "of the world," since we are one with Christ, Who is not of the world (John 17:14), and have received His Spirit which the "world cannot receive because it neither sees Him nor knows Him" (John 14:17). This life in spirit and in truth, this life in God, which we live while remaining in the world, does not diminish our appreciation for the reality of the creation with which God has surrounded us. It makes it more real for us, because we now see all ordinary created things in a new light. We see them and know them and love them in Christ. We see them in God and love them for His sake, and we know that "every creature of God is good, for it is sanctified" in Christ (I Timothy 4:4) and indeed has its very existence in Him and by Him. For "in Him all things hold together" (Colossians 2:17).

Our escape from Pharao and from Egypt is therefore not an escape from a material universe which is regarded as evil, but an escape from the blindness and illusion and evil that were in our own heart, and which made us unable to see and appreciate the good that is in the world, and even the true good that is in ourselves.

Christ delivers us from ourselves in order that we may find Him in ourselves. Our journey to Him is a journey into the depths of our own reality and into the reality that is all around us. As St. Bernard would say: *"Usque ad temetipsum occurre Deo tuo."*[1] Translated freely, this means that if we would find our God we must first find our true selves.

The whole sacramental economy by which God intervenes in the world in order to "separate" or "sanctify" His Chosen People for Himself, is expressed in the mysterious image of the Book of Wisdom in which the Church sees a figure of the Incarnation:

While all things were in quiet silence and the night was in the midst of her course, Thy almighty word leaped down from heaven from Thy royal throne as a fierce conqueror into the midst of the land ... and standing on the earth he reached even to heaven (Wisdom 18:14-15).

This description of the destroying angel is rightly applied to the Incarnation in the liturgy since he came not only to destroy the enemies of the people of God but to liberate those whose doorposts were marked by the Blood of the Paschal Lamb. Hence

---

[1] St. Bernard, *Sermon 1 for Advent*, n. 10.

this tremendous picture has a very intimate relation to our eucharistic communion with God. It reminds us that our communions are interventions by which God enters into our souls with His irresistible power in order to give our lives a whole new dimension by incorporating us into Himself, and making us His people.

When Elias was fleeing from Jezabel, he lay down under a tree in the wilderness and longed for death.

And he cast himself down and slept in the shadow of the juniper and behold an angel of the Lord touched him, and said: arise and eat! He looked, and behold there was at his hand a hearth cake and a vessel of water; and he ate and drank and fell asleep again. And the angel of the Lord came a second time, and touched him and said to him: arise and eat: for thou hast yet a great way to go. And he arose and ate, and walked in the strength of that food forty days and forty nights unto the mount of God, Horeb (III Kings 19:5-8).

So God intervened in the life of Elias at this crisis in his career, sent him miraculous food and drink, and then led him a forty days' journey through the desert to the mountain where the prophet heard the divine voice, and received his definitive mission. So too, in the Blessed Eucharist, the Logos intervenes in our lives, gives them a new meaning, a direction we could never have chosen or imagined, and leads us to the fulfillment of our vocation.

Every Communion therefore is a "viaticum"—it is food and drink to sustain us in our journey toward God. But while ordinary food and drink only supports our bodily life, this food is also our guide on our journey. For Jesus Who gives Himself to us in the Eucharist is "the way, the truth and the life" (John 14:6). As St. Bernard says: "He is the way that leads to truth; He is the Truth who promises life, and He is the Life which He Himself gives."[2] St. Augustine adds: "If you seek the truth, keep to the right way; for the way itself is the same as the truth ... you come through Christ to Christ ... through Christ the Man to Christ as God."[3]

The Israelites were ordered to eat the Paschal Lamb standing up, dressed for a journey; "You shall gird your reins, and you shall have shoes on your feet, holding staves in your hands, and you shall eat in haste, for it is the Phase (that is, the Passage) of the Lord" (Exodus 12:11). The Pasch, type of the true sacrifice which the Church offers in the Mass, and figure of the communion in which we are nourished by the mystical Lamb, was to be kept by the chosen people with an "everlasting observance" as a memorial of that intervention of

---

[2] "Ego sum via quae ad veritatem duco; ego sum veritas quae vitam promitto; ego sum vita, quam do." *De Gradibus Humilitatis,* i. 1.

[3] *Tractatus XIII in Joannem,* n. 4.

God by which they were delivered from Egypt. It was to be for them a perpetual reminder of Who God is. The Mass perpetuates for us the great "intervention" of God in our world by His Incarnation, Passion, Death and Resurrection, and keeps ever before our mind the fact that He is a God of power and of mercy, who has delivered us from the flesh and given us the freedom of His sons. He has made us His People and called us to journey to seek Him in the Promised Land of Heaven.

2. The Bread of God

The manna by which the Chosen People were nourished in the wilderness was a figure of the Eucharist, the spiritual food by which we are sustained and illuminated in the desert of this world.

Jesus, in His discourse on the Bread of Life in the synagogue of Capharnaum (John 6) proclaimed that He was the true manna, the "food that endures for life everlasting," the "Bread of God which came down from heaven and which gives life to the world" (John 6:27, 33).

The extraordinary richness of this chapter, which

is one of the greatest in the Gospels, cannot be appreciated unless we see in it the different levels of meaning by which Jesus makes clear that the Bread of Life is first of all His own Person, then His communication of Himself to us in two forms: in the Scriptures, the "word of God," and in the Eucharist.

The whole work of man in this life is to find God. We are not to labor for perishing food, but for the food of eternal life, the Logos. "This is the work of God, that you believe in Him Whom He has sent" (v.29). The Jews challenge Him to prove He is the Messias, by working a miracle. Moses prayed to God and manna was given to feed the people of Israel in the desert. What sign would Jesus give, to prove His claims? Jesus answers that what they need is not more external signs from Him, but faith in the depths of their own hearts. They have already seen a miracle in which He fed five thousand men with a few barley loaves and some little fishes: but that has done nothing to open their eyes: "I am the Bread of Life" says Jesus. "He who comes to me shall not hunger and he who believes in me shall never thirst. But I have told you that you have seen me and do not believe" (v.35–36).

All the sacraments, and especially the Eucharist, are protestations of our faith in the Son of God. If they are not an expression of our faith, then we

97

defile their truth with a lie. The discourse in which Jesus bluntly told the Jews that they could not be saved unless they ate His Flesh and drank His Blood was deliberately intended to surprise them, to shock them in the highest degree and indeed to scandalize them. It was necessary for the Jews to realize that they did not possess the true light, as they thought: on the contrary, the Law, the Scriptures, traditions of the elders which they believed to be sources of light and life were, in fact, blinding the eyes of their spirit and stifling the true life in their hearts, because these hearts refused to open themselves to the Spirit of God.

He told them: "You search the Scriptures because in them you think that you have life everlasting. And it is they that bear witness to me, yet you are not willing to come to me that you may have life" (John 5:39-40).

And to the Scribes, the learned men, He said: "Woe to you scribes, for you have taken away the key of knowledge; you have not entered yourselves, and those who were entering you have hindered" (Luke 11:52).

The interventions of God in the lives of men have nothing to do with formalism and pietistic routine. God comes to us always to "make all things new" (Apocalypse 21:5) and each time He comes it is necessary for us, in some sense, to leave all and to follow Him. Therefore we cannot too often emphasize this "dynamic" character of the

Eucharist, in which Christ comes to us as a force uprooting our minds and wills from this world and transporting us with Himself "out of this world to the Father" (John 13:1).

In receiving Communion, it is not sufficient merely to perform a soulless, external action. There must be an interior movement of our will which takes us out of ourselves at least in desire. We are familiar with the fact that Christ "comes to us" in Communion, but we forget the far more important aspect of this great mystery: in order for Him to come to us, we must "come to Him," we must allow ourselves "to be drawn to Him" by the Father. That is to say, in our communions we must try to be conscious that we are *yielding ourselves to the divine action* which draws us into the mystery of Christ. We must realize that in seeking Jesus we are obeying the will of the Father and the secret inspirations of the Holy Spirit urging us on to eternal life as members of Christ. "This is the will of the Father, that whoever beholds the Son and believes in Him, shall have everlasting life" (John 6:40). We who seek to behold the face of Christ are aware, by that very fact, that we are among those whom the Father has "given" to His Son. "This is the will of Him that sent me, the Father, that I should lose nothing of what He has given me but that I should raise it up on the last day" (id. 39). "All that the Father gives to me will come to

99

me, and he that comes to me I will not cast out"
(id. 37).

In yielding ourselves to the will of the Father we
are in fact obeying the same power which Jesus
obeys in coming to us. Our Communion is therefore a union with the will of the Eternal Father,
and a participation in the same mystery of God with
Christ the Incarnate Word. As Word, He is of one
will with the Father by nature. By our Communion
with Him we become one will and one Spirit with
the Father by charity. Charity identifies us with
the Son Who said He would not cast us out because, as He said, "I have come down from heaven
to do not my own will but the will of Him that
sent me, and this is the will of the Father, that I
should lose nothing of what He has given me" (id.
38–39).

Jesus adds: "No one can come to me unless the
Father who sent me draw him. . . . Everyone who
has listened to the Father and has learned, comes to
me" (Id. 44, 45). Here Jesus quotes Isaias, who
prophesied that in the Messianic times "they shall
all be taught by God" (Isaias 54:13).

All through the High Priestly prayer of Jesus in
the seventeenth chapter of St. John, Our Lord
speaks to the Father of those "whom the Father
has given to Him."

Father the hour has come, glorify thy son that thy
Son may glorify thee, even as thou hast given him

power over all flesh, in order that *to all thou hast given him* He may give everlasting life.... I have manifested Thy name *to the men whom thou hast given me out of the world. They were thine, and thou hast given them to me* and they have kept thy word. Now they have learnt that whatever thou has given me is from thee....

I pray for those whom thou hast given me, for they are thine and all things that are mine are thine, and thine are mine, and I am glorified in them....Father, I will that where I am they also whom thou hast given me may be with me in order that they may behold my glory which thou hast given me because thou hast loved me before the creation of the world (John 17:2, 6-8, 9, 10, 24).

We are not sufficiently conscious of this aspect of our communions. We think of them perhaps only as ritual acts of devotion with which we seek to please God, to offer Him homage and gain merit for our souls. Those things are true indeed. But let us look deeper, and we will discover that we are face to face with the mystery of God's love for our souls—we are confronted by our own ineffable and mysterious personal vocation to become "other Christs"—we face the fact that this Communion is the sign that *we belong to God*, that we are *His possession*, His chosen ones, and for that reason He comes to us and gives Himself to us as *our* possession.

We also think far too little of the fact that in communion we are freely uniting ourselves with the supreme designs of God's will for ourselves, committing ourselves in the highest and most perfect sense to His all-wise Providence, and carying out the purposes of His love more fully than could be possible in any other way. We are not only performing a supremely pure act of adoration of the divine Being, but much more we are entering into the plan of God's will to "re-establish all things in Christ." It is in the act of abandoning ourselves to this salvific will that the eyes of our soul are opened at last to understand the full meaning of God's love for us in the mystery of Christ. In order to please God perfectly, we must receive this illumination.

The mystery of our incorporation in Christ and of our life in Him is at the same time a mystery of self-abandonment and of enlightenment. Baptism is the life-giving sacrament that makes us part of His Mystical Body, and it is also the sacrament of illumination. The Eucharist brings to perfection the work of enlightenment and of life in Christ that is begun by the other sacraments. It is God's will that we be enlightened by Christ since in fact the giving of supernatural light and the communication of supernatural life are inseparable in His designs. "This is eternal life, to know thee the one true God, and Jesus Christ Whom thou hast sent" (John 17:3). Therefore "He has called us out of darkness into His admirable light" (I Peter 2:9) and "God Who has commanded light to shine out of darkness has shone in our hearts to give enlightenment concerning the knowledge of the glory of God shining on the face of Christ Jesus" (II Corinthians 4:6).

The whole Gospel of St. John is the record of the light of God struggling with the darkness of the world, the victory of the Logos over death so that men may come to Him and have life and light. In Him, the transcendent life and light which are His very nature quicken and enlighten men. "In Him was life, and the life was the light of men, and the light shines in the darkness and the darkness grasped it not.... He was the true light that enlightens every man that comes into the world.... He came into His own and His own received Him not" (John 1:4, 5, 9, 11). All through the fourth Gospel Christ repeats His complaint that men love darkness rather than light (John 3:10), and we have seen that those who most loved darkness were the ones who searched the Scriptures and thought they were in full possession of the light (John 5:39–40).

To know Christ, the Logos, is to "receive Him" and to receive Him is to become a son of God. This regeneration is the work of faith and of baptism. We become sons of God by being born "not of blood, nor of the will of the flesh, nor of the will of men, but of God" (John 1:13), and "unless a

man be born again of water and the Spirit he cannot enter the kingdom of God" (John 3:5). Jesus
had to rebuke Nicodemus, a "master in Israel" who
though he had studied the Law and the prophets
was ignorant of this all-important spiritual truth
(John 3:10). Now this supernatural life is communicated to us only through and by Christ. He is the
"light of the world" and whoever follows Him
does not walk in darkness, but has the light of life
(John 8:12). Therefore Jesus tells us: "While you
have the light, believe in the light that you may
become the sons of light" (John 12:36).

Can we say that we walk in the light when we
do not really know Him? Even at the Last Supper
Jesus rebuked the disciples because they did not yet
know Him. For if they had known Him, Philip
would not have asked that He show them the
Father. "Have I been so long a time with you and
you have not known me? Philip, He who sees me
sees also the Father . . . Dost thou not believe that
I am in the Father and the Father in me?" (John
14:9, 10). And to Thomas He said: "I am the way,
the truth and the Life, no one comes to the Father
but through me. If you had known me you would
have known the Father also. And henceforth you
do know Him, and have seen Him" (John 14:6-7).

This brings us back again to the eucharistic discourse in St. John, and to the "will of the Father"
that we be united to Christ, enlightened by Him,

so that we know the Father in Him. It is only when we see that the Father is in Christ and Christ in the Father that we really grasp the mystery of the Bread of Life. "As the living Father has sent me, and I live because of the Father, so he that eats me shall live because of me" (John 6:58). Just as the Son is generated eternally in the bosom of the Father, so we whom the Father has given to the Son, if we live by the Son must live forever (John 6:59).

The life which Christ gives to the world is the life which He receives from the Father, the life of the Father in Him. We need see no further than Christ Himself in order to "see" the invisible source of Life. The simplicity of the Gospels, if kept in mind, makes false mysticism impossible. Christ has delivered us forever from the esoteric and strange. He has brought the light of God to our own level to transfigure our ordinary existence.

The invisible God has become man in order that we may see Him and, through the man Christ, come to know the eternal Father. But once again this is more than a matter of speculation. It is by doing the will of Christ that we come to know the Father. "He who has my commandments and keeps them, he it is who loves me. . . . If anyone loves me he will keep my word and my Father will love him and we will come to Him and make our abode with him" (John 14:21, 23). But what is the will of

Christ? That we love one another. "A new commandment I give you, that you love one another: that as I have loved you, you also love one another" (John 13:34). This is not a new theme, but part of the same idea. It is by loving one another that we are incorporated in Christ, enlightened by Christ.

If we do not love one another, we cannot eat the Bread of Life, we cannot come to the Father. It is only by loving one another that we allow the Father to draw us to Christ, for it is by love that we become one Mystical Body, one Christ. And only by "being Christ" can we come to the knowledge of Christ. This last thought is central in St. Augustine's commentary on the eucharistic discourse. "The faithful know the Body of Christ if they do not neglect to *be* the Body of Christ. Let them become the Body of Christ if they want to live by the Spirit of Christ: for only the Body of Christ lives by the Spirit of Christ."[4]

Here we begin to see the inseparable connection between the Eucharist and the Church. Both have been called the "Mystical Body of Christ." Indeed, in patristic times it was the privilege of the Church to be called simply the "Body of Christ" without

---

[4] Norunt fideles corpus Christi si corpus Christi esse non negligant: fiant corpus Christi si volunt vivere de Spiritu Christi: de Spiritu Christi non vivit nisi Corpus Christi. St. Augustine, *Tractatus xxvi in Joannem*.

any qualification, while the term *corpus mysticum* was applied to the Eucharist, a fact that reminds us that the Church is the "reality" *(res)* which is signified by the Blessed Sacrament.

The fact that the Fathers so often speak of our unity in Christ rather than of the Eucharist itself, when they speak of the Blessed Sacrament, should not lead us to imagine that they thought the Eucharist was only a symbol. They were too well acquainted with the Scriptures to think any such thing, and indeed Jesus makes it quite clear that the Eucharist is in all truth His sacred Body and Blood. "I am the living Bread that comes down from heaven . . . the bread that I will give is my flesh, for the life of the world" (John 6:52). And when the Jews complained that this was impossible, instead of explaining his words as symbolic, Jesus insisted on their literal meaning, without however revealing the sacramental mode in which He would give His flesh to be our food. "Amen, amen I say unto you, unless you eat the flesh of the Son of man and drink His blood, you shall not have life in you. He who eats my flesh and drinks my blood has life everlasting, and I will raise him up the last day. For my flesh is food indeed and my blood is drink indeed. He who eats my flesh and drinks my blood, abides in me and I in him" (John 6:54–57).

However Jesus gives us His Body not merely as the principle of our own individual life and sanctification, but as the principle of unity in His Mystical Body. He unites us not only to Himself, not only to the Father in Himself but also to one another. This is the full "Mystery" of the Eucharist, and we must always look at the Blessed Sacrament in the light of these implications. We must always see the Mystery as a whole. We must see the "whole Christ," the *Res Sacramenti*, for without our unity in charity the Blessed Sacrament would lack its real meaning.

St. Paul gives the complete view of the Blessed Sacrament, the real presence as well as the *Res Sacramenti*, when he says: "And the bread that we break, is it not the partaking of the Body of the Lord? Because the bread is one, we though many are one body, all of us who partake of the one bread" (I Corinthians 10:16–17). Here we see that both the Eucharist and the Church are the Body of Christ, and the Eucharist is the principle of the unity which holds us together in one Spirit, in perfect charity.

In His High Priestly prayer, Jesus tells us the whole meaning of our unity in Him; "I in them and Thou (Father) in me, that they may be perfected in unity, and that the world may know that Thou hast loved them as Thou hast loved me" (John 17:23).

St. Cyril of Alexandria sums up the meaning of the words "I am the Bread of Life" in a succinct formula. *Verbum secundum naturam vita, cuncta vivificans.* "The Word, being Life in His very nature, gives life to all things.... He is generated by the living Father... and since the function of that which is life by nature is to give life to all things, Christ gives life to all."[5]

3. Communion and Its Effects

Let us now consider in more detail the fruits of Communion in the individual soul, before going on to consider the unity of all the faithful in Christ as the chief effect of the Eucharist.

First of all, how does the Blessed Eucharist produce its fruit in us?

When a soul that is properly disposed receives this Sacrament, it comes into contact with the Logos, the Word of Life, and is by that very fact filled with spiritual life. Christ instituted this Sacrament precisely in order that He might unite Himself to each one of us as the source of all life and strength and light and spiritual fecundity. He comes to us in this Sacrament in such a way that

[5] *In Joannis Evangelium,* lib. 3, c.6.

He can be entirely present in each one who receives Him, and present at the same time in all. Hence He comes first of all to unite us to Himself as members to their Head, in one Mystical Body. All the other fruits of the Sacrament flow from this one, which is the most important. This is the chief reason for the real presence of Christ in the Eucharist. The Body of Christ is present as a substance, under the accidents of bread, so that He may be able to give Himself undivided to each one who receives a consecrated Host and so be present at the same time in them all.

Now the Body of Christ which we receive in the Blessed Eucharist is the living Body of the Incarnate Word. Acting therefore as an instrument of the divine nature, this Body of Christ comes to us filled with the power and the reality of the Logos and of the Holy Spirit. When we receive the Blessed Eucharist, our souls are filled with the Spirit of God and we are as intimately united to the Logos as if He were the soul of our own soul and the being of our own being. Scheeben says:

The flesh of Christ is to nourish us not as mere natural flesh but as flesh steeped in the Spirit of God unto a life that is at once divine and spiritual. . . . What meat and drink are to the body, that the light of truth and glory and the fiery torrent of love are to the soul. . . . In the sacrament of Christ's blood the Spirit of divine life, gushing from the Logos like the blood from

His bodily heart, pours into our souls as the blood of divine life, to anoint them and to allay their thirst. . . . The divinity of the Logos is truly the *panis superessentialis* which is concealed under the substance of the body present in the Eucharist.[6]

It is by this outpouring of divine life in our souls that Christ unites us most perfectly to His Sacrifice. The charity that is communicated to us in the Eucharist by the Heart of the Divine Savior is at once the formal and efficient cause of the love which it arouses in our own hearts. And our response of charity is like a flame communicated to us by the Divine Victim burning in the fire of the Holy Spirit. United to Him, we are consumed in the glory of one and the same flame. Scheeben continues in the spirit of the Fathers:

Made godlike by the hypostatic union and steeped in the Holy Spirit, it is this flesh which is to arouse a truly spiritual disposition of sacrifice in us, and pour forth the consuming fire of love into our souls. It is from this flesh that we are to draw the strength to offer our souls up to God; and in union with the flesh which reposes in the bosom of the Godhead we are to lay our souls as a worthy and sweet-smelling sacrifice before the throne of God. The flesh of Christ must scent our souls through and through with the sweet aroma of the Holy Spirit, with which it is filled itself, so that they may become truly spiritual and

---

[6] *The Mysteries of Christianity*, p. 520, 524 (footnote).

divine, and may send up a most pleasing incense to God.[7]

In uniting us to His Sacrifice, Jesus therefore wills first of all to fill us with the same Holy Spirit of love with which He is filled Himself, and here we see once again the whole meaning of the Eucharist. Jesus comes to us in this divine mystery in order to divinize us and transform us entirely in Himself. The Fathers never looked at the Eucharist otherwise than as the way to the highest mystical union with God.

The Canticle of Canticles, which is the nuptial song of the wedding of the Logos with humanity, is applied by St. Ambrose especially to our union with Christ in the Eucharist. He says:

You have therefore come to the altar and you have received the grace of Christ, His heavenly sacraments. The Church rejoices in the redemption of so many and exults with spiritual joy at the sight of the white-robed family. (He is addressing the newly baptized, who have received the Eucharist for the first time.) You will find all this in the Canticle of Canticles. In her joy the Church cries out to Christ, for she has a banquet all prepared which is splendid enough to be the banquet of heaven itself. Hence she says: "Let my Brother come down into His garden and pluck the fruits of His trees" (Canticle 5:1). What are these fruit trees? You had become dry wood in Adam, but now, having

---

[7] *Ibid.*, pp. 520-521.

been made fruit trees in Christ, you are bearing your harvest. And the Lord Jesus gladly accepts this invitation, and replies to His Church with a kindness that belongs to heaven: "I have come down," He says, "into my garden. I have harvested my myrrh and my aromatical balsams. I have eaten my bread with my honey and I have drunk my wine with my milk." "Eat, my brothers," He says, "and be glad with wine" (Canticle, *ibid.*).[8]

The saint goes on to show how the wine with which we are gladdened is the Holy Spirit, for every time we receive the Eucharist we are cleansed of our sins and inebriated by the Spirit of God, according to the injunction of the Apostle who told us not to be drunk with wine but with the Holy Spirit. St. Ambrose adds: "He who is drunk with wine, staggers. But he who is inebriated by the Spirit is rooted in Christ. It is then a good inebriation, which produces sobriety in the soul." It is clear that among the most precious fruits of Holy Communion are the joy and purity of heart that flow from an intimate, quasi-physical union with the Word made Flesh, and that every Communion can bring to us the *sobria ebrietas* of which we read everywhere in the Fathers. St. Cyprian, for example, describes it in greater detail. He argues that wine must be offered in the sacrifice and not

---

[8] *De Sacramentis*, V, 14-15.

water, because water does not symbolize blood and does not inebriate.

The chalice of the Lord inebriates men in such a way that they become sober. It brings their minds to heavenly wisdom so that each one loses his taste for this world and awakens to the understanding of God. And just as ordinary wine gladdens the mind and relaxes the soul and drives out all sorrow, so when we have drunk the Blood of the Lord and the saving chalice the memory of the old man is put out of our mind and we forget about our former conduct in the world, and the sad, dejected heart which was burdened with sins and anxieties, is filled with the happiness of divine pardon.[9]

This "sobriety" is nothing else but the sign of our transformation in Christ. For the Living Bread, when we receive it, transforms us into itself and is not absorbed by our bodies as ordinary food. True, the species of bread dissolve within us, but the substance of the Logos becomes the nourishment of our souls in such a way that we live no longer by our own life but by His. "This is the bread that has come down from heaven; not as your fathers ate the manna and died. He who eats this bread shall live forever. . . . It is the Spirit that gives life. The flesh profits nothing" (John 6:59, 64).

---

[9] *Epistola* 63, XI.

While not touching on the question of mystical grace, Pope Pius XII describes our union with Christ in the Eucharist in much the same language:

The very nature of the Sacrament demands that its reception should produce rich fruits of Christian sanctity.... Therefore let us all enter into the closest union with Christ and strive to lose ourselves as it were in His most Holy Soul, and so be united to Him that we may have a share in those acts in which He adores the Blessed Trinity with a homage that is most acceptable and by which He offers to the eternal Father supreme praise and thanks which find an harmonious echo throughout the heavens and earth, according to the words of the prophet: "All ye works of the Lord, bless ye the Lord."[10]

We need not fear to multiply quotations and authorities in speaking of this great mystery. Since the Eucharist is the very heart of Christian life and Christian mysticism, and since all our joy and all our strength are found in the Sacramental Christ, Who opens to us the way by which we return to Paradise, it is fitting that we meditate on the words in which the Church herself proposes to us this teaching in her solemn and ordinary magisteria.

The Council of Florence teaches us that the Holy Eucharist produces in our souls all the effects that material food produces in our bodies. It brings us

---

[10] *Mediator Dei*, N.C.W.C. translation, #127.

spiritual nourishment, promotes our spiritual growth, refreshes and heals our souls, repairing their losses, and finally it brings spiritual delight: we are drawn away from evil, strengthened in the good, and attain to a new growth in grace and virtue. All this is brought about not only by our loving memory of Christ but by our actual union with Him, our incorporation in Him by grace and our union with His other members in the fervor of charity.[11]

The Council of Trent reminds us that Christ is received in this Sacrament as a remedy and antidote for sin, delivering us from the faults of human frailty which beset us every day and preserving us from falling into mortal sin. St. Ignatius of Antioch had gone further, and called the Blessed Sacrament the medicine of immortality—*pharmacum immortalitatis*, and the Council of Trent incorporates this idea in the same chapter, teaching that the Eucharist is "a pledge of future glory and of everlasting happiness."[12]

In the very same breath the council adds that the "Eucharist is the symbol of that Body of which He is the Head and to which He willed that we should be joined as members by the closest possible union of faith, hope and charity."

These familiar texts, quoted in all the manuals of

[11] *Decretum pro Armenis*, DB. 698.
[12] Session XIII Cap.2, DB. 875.

theology, often fail to reveal their full meaning. They should be pondered in silent prayer. The truths they contain are of the very highest importance, and of incalculable consequences in our spiritual life and pastoral activity. The Council says that the Eucharist is a remedy for sin, but does not by any means say that it is *merely* a remedy for sin. The Sacrament is a pledge of future glory and as such it gives us something of the joy of heaven even here and now, though in the obscurity of theological hope. It brings us not only the grace of a most intimate union with Christ as the Head of the Mystical Body, but also unites us with the other members of the Body. To be more precise, it imparts to us as a sacramental grace that fervor of charity by which we can, if we make good use of it, unite ourselves more firmly to Christ and to our brethren. We ought to realize that our union with the Mystical Christ, that is with the members as well as the Head, is an integral part of our eucharistic life and a most important aspect of it. It is through our union with the members that we receive consolation and strength, as well as directly from Christ Himself.

The presence of Christ within us, "the author of the sacraments and the fountain head of all sacraments and heavenly gifts,"[13] becomes a spring of

---

[13] *Catechismus Concilii Tridentini*, II, iv, q.45.

living water welling up into life everlasting, a permanent principle of charity and a source of fervent love which seeks to translate itself into Christian action and praise of God. The grace of the Eucharist is not confined to the moments of thanksgiving after Mass and communion, but reaches out into our whole day and into all the affairs of our life, in order to sanctify and transform them in Christ.[14]

The Fathers of the Church loved to dwell on the fact that Christ, present in us as the source of all life, comes to us in Communion not only to give us a pledge of future life but also to prepare our souls and bodies for the general resurrection. This effect of the Eucharist is not so much a physical consequence of contact with His risen and transfigured flesh as a side effect of the charity poured out into our souls by the Logos, and by the hope of resurrection which flows from the presence of Christ within us. St. Irenaeus says:

Just as the bread which is produced by the earth hears the invocation of the Holy Spirit and ceases to be bread in order to become the Eucharist, made of two elements, earthly and celestial, so too our bodies, receiving the Eucharist are now no longer corruptible, for they possess the hope of the resurrection.[15]

All these thoughts on the Eucharist make it clear to us that in this Sacrament, in which He not only

---

[14] Cf *Mediator Dei*, #128.
[15] *Contra Haereses*, IV, 18, 5.

gives grace to us but also gives Himself, we are led to a supreme peak of spiritual fulfillment. This Sacrament is not given to us merely in order that we do something, but that we may *be* someone: that we may be Christ. That we may be perfectly identified with Him. Comparing the Eucharist with confirmation, St. Thomas says that confirmation brings us an increase of grace in order to resist temptation, but the Eucharist does even more: it increases and perfects our spiritual life itself, in order that we may be perfected in our own being, our own personality, by *our union with God: per hoc sacramentum augetur gratia et perficitur spiritualis vita ad hoc quod homo in seipso perfectus existat per conjunctionem ad Deum.*[16] In other words, by our union with Christ in the Eucharist we find our true selves. The false self, the "old man" is burned away by the fervor of charity generated by His intimate presence within our soul. And the "new man" comes into full possession of himself as we "live, now not we, but Christ liveth in us."

This explains why it is sometimes difficult or even impossible for some truly fervent souls to converse with Christ within themselves after communion by words and "acts" as if He were a separate person. Their union with Him is in fact deeper

---

[16] *Summa Theologica*, III, Q.79, a.1, ad 1.

than that, and much closer. So close is He to them that they can no longer distinguish Him clearly through concepts. But so close is He that they no longer remain aware of themselves. What is left for them? Must they seek to see themselves clearly, or to see Him? Not at all. In the words of Pope Pius XII which we have just quoted, they would do better to "lose themselves in His Holy Soul." They would do better to let the Spirit carry them away, so that they lose all sense of the distinction between themselves and Him and are momentarily absorbed in the tremendous reality of His presence which defies analysis and of which there is no adequate description. They would do better to rejoice in the *sobria ebrietas* mentioned by St. Ambrose. If we would use some text to meditate on, after Communion, there could hardly be anything better or more appropriate than the Canticle of Canticles, unless perhaps we were to chose some passage from the discourse at the Last Supper as it is recorded in St. John.

All these fruits of eucharistic Communion are set before us clearly and with rich detail in the prayers of the Sacred Liturgy. Everywhere the post-communions and secret prayers of the Mass remind us of this great mystery of renewal and transformation in Christ. In the Ordinary of the Mass the priest reflects after Communion that he has been "re-created by the pure and holy sacraments" (*quem pura et sancta refecerunt sacramenta)* and that what he has received as a "temporal gift" is to become for him an "eternal remedy" (and here again we hear the echoes of Ignatius of Antioch with his *"pharmacum immortalitatis."*) At the greatest feasts of the liturgical year, Christmas and Easter, the Church prays that we may be "purged of all our old life and may go on to become new creatures"[17] and that the Word of God's "new nativity in the flesh may set us free from the ancient yoke of sin."[18] Everywhere in the liturgical year we meet with expressions like: "We whom thou dost re-make with thy heavenly sacraments," "We whom Thou dost re-create in Thy sacred mysteries," and brief, vivid phrases so succinct as to be untranslatable: *cujus laetemur gustu, renovemur effectu.*

This transformation, however, is by no means perfect. The Sacrament brings us graces which we must use in order to increase our charity and gain eternal life. Sacramental grace is the means by which we carry out the work of our salvation and sanctification, the daily renewal of our "inner man" (II Corinthians 4:16). Hence the Eucharist cleanses us from sin and leads us to the heavenly kingdom"[19] and strengthens us so that "from day to

---

[17] Postcommunion, Easter Wednesday.
[18] Collect, Christmas, 3rd Mass.
[19] Postcommunion, Wednesday of the 4th week of Lent.

day it may gradually elevate our conduct to a level with the life of heaven" *(de die in die ad caelestis vitae transferat actionem).*[20]

Hence the sacramental graces of the Eucharist strengthen our weakness and help us to gain stability in virtue. By means of this Sacrament, God "guides our wavering hearts,"[21] makes us better able to restrain our unruly appetites[22] and keeps away from us all baneful powers.[23] The Eucharist defends us especially against the devil's attacks.[24]

In particular, the Eucharist helps us to avoid the specious attractions of error and makes us firm in our faith: *ut errorum circumventione depulsa, fidei firmitatem consequamur.*[25] It strengthens us in the love for Christ's Name,[26] and teaches us to despise earthly things and love the things of heaven.[27] It is no wonder then that the Eucharist is the food that strengthened the martyrs. Indeed the liturgy calls it "the sacrifice from which all martyrdom took its beginning."[28]

---

[20] Secret, Sunday within the Octave of Corpus Christi.

[21] "Nutantia corda tu dirigas." Secret, Wednesday 1st week of Lent.

[22] "Continentiae promptioris tribuat effectum." Secret, Friday after Ash Wednesday.

[23] Postcommunion, Friday in Passion Week.

[24] Secret, 15th Sunday after Pentecost.

[25] Collect, Feast of St. Justin Martyr (April 14).

[26] In tui Nominis amore roboremur—Common of Martyrs.

[27] Terrena despicere et amare caelestia—a frequent theme in liturgical orations.

[28] Secret, Thursday of the Third week of Lent.

It was by martyrdom that St. Ignatius of Antioch, St. Polycarp, St. Cyprian and others sought to consummate their eucharistic life and to "find Christ," and this fact is one of the most striking witnesses of the power of grace that is poured out on us in the Blessed Sacrament. We can close this chapter with the words in which St. Cyprian declares how important is the Eucharist for those who are to face martyrdom. He is speaking of the duty of the bishop to remain with his flock in time of persecution.

It is not to the dying, but to the living that we must give communion in order that we may not leave unarmed and naked those whom we exhort to battle, but may strengthen them with the protection of the Body and Blood of Christ. And since the purpose of the Eucharist is to defend those who receive it, we must provide those whom we wish to be safe from the adversary, with the protection of Holy Communion. For how shall we teach and urge them on to shed their blood in testimony to His Name, if, when they are about to go forth to battle for Christ, we deny them the blood of the Lord? Or how shall we make them ready for the chalice of martyrdom, if we do not at first admit them to drink the chalice of the Lord in Church...?[29]

For you must know and must believe for certain

---

[29] St. Cyprian, *Epistola synodica ad Cornelium Papam*, P.L. 3, 865.

that the day of persecution has begun to descend upon our heads, and the end of the world and the time of the antichrist, so that we must all stand ready for battle, and no one of us must think of anything except the glory of eternal life and the crown promised to those who confess the Name of the Lord. Nor let us think that the things that are to come will be like those with which we are already familiar. Far worse and far more savage is the struggle that is now upon us and the soldiers of Christ must prepare themselves with the purest faith and with dauntless courage, reminding themselves that the reason why they drink each day the chalice of the Blood of Christ is that they may shed their blood for Christ. This is what it means, to want to be found with Christ: to imitate the teachings and the actions of Christ, according to the words of John the Apostle: "He who says he remains in Christ must walk as Christ walked" and blessed Paul the Apostle exhorts and teaches us saying: "We are sons. If we are sons of God we are also heirs of God, co-heirs with Christ, provided that we suffer together with Him in order to be glorified with him."[30]

---

[30] *Epistola* 56, P.L. 4, 350.

V

O SACRUM CONVIVIUM

1. Come to the Marriage Feast!

Christ in the Gospels frequently compares the kingdom of heaven to a wedding feast. "The kingdom of heaven is like a king who made a marriage feast for his son" (Matthew 22:2). But in the parables of the feast, there is always difficulty in getting the guests to assemble. The King sends out his servants with the message: "Tell those who are invited, behold, I have prepared my dinner; my oxen and my fatlings are killed and everything is ready: come to the marriage feast." But the guests do not respond to the invitation. They have no desire to come to the wedding. The king persists in seeking guests to fill his banquet hall. He sends out servants again saying: "Go out quickly into the streets and the lanes of the city, and bring in here the poor and the crippled and the blind and the lame. . . . Go out into the highways and hedges and make them come in, so that my house may be filled" (Luke 14:21, 23).

Although these parables do not refer directly to the Eucharist, they have a definite bearing on the mystery. For the eucharistic banquet is the very heart and center of that Christian life which is to culminate in the banquet of heaven. Now we must remember that a banquet is not a banquet if it is attended by only one or two people. A feast is an occasion of joy for *many* people. Also, a feast is of such a nature that it draws people to itself, and makes them leave everything else in order to participate in its joys. To feast together is to bear witness to the joy one has at being with his friends. The mere act of eating together, quite apart from a banquet or some other festival occasion, is by its very nature a sign of friendship and of "communion."

In modern times we have lost sight of the fact that even the most ordinary actions of our every day life are invested, by their very nature, with a deep spiritual meaning. The table is in a certain sense the center of family life, the expression of family life. Here the children gather with their parents to eat the food which the love of their parents has provided. At table the children gratefully share in the labors and sacrifices of their parents. The common meal is blessed by the father's prayers and enlivened by the conversation of the whole family. In this common act, the family takes cognizance of itself as a family, becomes as it were conscious of its own proper existence and dignity and vitality. The meal of a Christian family is not so much a mere satisfaction of bodily needs as the celebration of a mystery of charity, the mystery of the Christian home. And this mystery is already very deep, for Christ Himself is present in the union of husband and wife and in the children of the sanctified union. It is Christ Who feeds those present and brings them all the other blessings without which life would be impossible or at least miserable.

So, too, with a banquet. The Latin word *convivium* contains more of this mystery than our words "banquet" or "feast." To call a feast a *"convivium"* is to call it a "mystery of the sharing of life"—a mystery in which guests partake of the good things prepared and given to them by the love of their host, and in which the atmosphere of friendship and gratitude expands into a sharing of thoughts and sentiments, and ends in common rejoicing. In the perspective of ancient wisdoms, as well as of Christian charity, the guest is regarded as an envoy of God, an angel in disguise. The host in turn is an image of God the Father. In the Christian context, guests and hosts together are a sign of the rejoicing of the "One Christ loving Himself."

In our day in which the individualism of the bourgeois nineteenth century has corrupted its way into totalitarian submersion of the individual in the masses, this healthy natural consciousness of the *convivium*—the sharing of a common life and interests by a small group which is really united by a spontaneous and instinctive sympathy, has yielded to the vast, amorphous anonymity of the mass meeting. Respect for a common life in which many individual persons come together to offer their various contributions to the common joys and sorrows and responsibilities of all has given place to the servile need for a "mass" society in which one man violently imposes his own views and opinions on the whole collectivity. Men are not asked to contribute anything but servile conformity and applause. Totalitarian society systematically dissolves the firm bonds which unite men in the basic social units—families and parochial communities—in order to uproot the individual from spontaneous human attachments and transplant him into organizations focused upon the cult of the totality and of its aspirations, embodied in the leader. Every kind of pressure is brought to bear upon the individual to divest him of his true personality and of his normal social attachments. He is systematically made to distrust and fear other individuals, and to shift his confidence from those with whom he lives—from concrete persons of flesh and blood— to a leader whom he never sees or hears at close range, but only on the radio or on the screen at the movies. Love is destroyed and replaced by fanaticism. What is true of totalitarian states is true to a lesser degree, but true, nevertheless, of the great capitalist democracies in which the same processes take place, more slowly, less systematically, but none the less surely, under the pressure of an ever growing materialistic technocracy.

In such a time as ours it is therefore most important to remember that the Eucharist is a *convivium*, a sacred banquet. It is the celebration in which the Christian family, the Church, rejoices together at a common table with the Apostles and all the saints and all believers. It is neither a purely individual, purely subjective encounter with God on the one hand, nor is it on the other hand a mass meeting, a kind of enormous religious rally, in which the totality of the faithful is conscious of nothing more than its own totality.

Communion is a *sacrum convivium*. It is a banquet in which the faithful not only enjoy, personally, the spiritual benefits and satisfactions of union with the eucharistic Christ, but also become aware of their common participation in the divine life. The joy of Communion is something that we share with one another. And this sharing is not merely psychological, it is one of the objective spiritual fruits of the Sacrament. The Eucharist is the Sacrament of charity, the *sacramentum unitatis*, the Sacrament of our union in Christ. Consciousness of this unity, of this sharing of the life of Christ, is necessary if the Eucharist is to fulfill its function as a perfect sacrifice of praise for the honor and glory of God.

Let us listen to the voice of the Church. The Council of Trent tells us that the Sacrament of the Eucharist in which Jesus left to His Church the fullness of His love for men, is not only the spiritual food by which we are strengthened and purified of sin, not only the Sacrament in which we live by the very life of Christ Himself, not only a pledge of future glory but also it is the "symbol of that one Body of His, of which He is the Head, and to which He would have us be joined as members by the closest bonds of faith, hope and charity, in order that we may all "say the same thing and that there may be no dissensions among us" (Cf I Corinthians 1:10).[1]

In the language of St. Thomas Aquinas, the *res sacramenti*, or spiritual reality which is signified and effected by the Holy Eucharist, is the union of the faithful in charity. *Res hujus sacramenti est unitas corporis mystici sine qua non potest esse*

---

[1] Session XIII cap. 2, DB. 875.

salus.[2] The sacramental reception of the Body of Christ would not attain its principal effects if we were not, by our communion with the Incarnate Word, united to the Mystical Christ, the Church. It would be of little value for an individual to be united to the Head of the Mystical Body if he were not, by that fact also, united with the members. There is no *vita* without the *convivium.* Christianity is not only a *contact with* Christ but an *incorporation* into the whole Christ.

In the Eucharist, Jesus has given us the only perfectly satisfactory means of fulfilling the great commandment which He left us at the same time as He instituted the Sacrament. "A new commandment I give to you, that you love one another. That as I have loved you, you also love one another" (John 13:34). For in the Blessed Eucharist Jesus has given us the supreme expression of that love by which He Himself loved us, the love with which He Himself is loved by the Father and with which we are to love one another.

The "new commandment" is the summary and crown of all the Scriptures. In those three words "love one another" are included all the other teachings of the Old and New Testaments, for, as Paul tells us, "The whole Law is fulfilled in one word: thou shalt love thy neighbor as thyself" (Galatians

---

[2] Summa Theologica, III, Q.73, a.3.

5:14), and "Love is the fulfillment of the Law" (Romans 13:10). But Jesus completed His teaching by giving us, in the Blessed Sacrament, more than words could ever contain or convey: His very self, His own love, His divine Spirit communicated to the depths of our soul by His soul and His Body. The purpose of both the commandment and of the Sacrament is the same: that by loving one another we should be one as Christ and the Father are one (John 17:21–22).

Much as Jesus loves us, His love for us and His desire for personal union with our souls is not the end of this Sacrament. What is intended above all is the glory of the Father. The glory of God is God Himself, and our unity in the charity of Christ is the most perfect external manifestation of the hidden glory of God. For by selfless charity we reproduce on earth, and in time, the circumincession of the Three Divine Persons, each in the others, which is the glory and the joy of the Blessed in eternity because it is the joy of God Himself. Hence if we wish to enter deeply into the mystery of the Eucharist, we must realize and appreciate a "reality" which goes beyond the Real Presence of Christ under the sacramental species and which is the ultimate reason for that Real Presence.

2. The Eucharist and the Church

We will never appreciate the Real Presence fully until we see the intimate connection which exists between the Mystery of the Eucharist and the Mystery of the Church, two sacred realities which completely interpenetrate to form a single whole; Mysteries which, when separated, elude the grasp of our spirit altogether. For we will never really appreciate the Eucharist or the Church if we conceive them to be two entirely different "bodies of Christ." There are not really two bodies of Christ. It is in a sense quite true to say that there is only one *Corpus Mysticum.* There is one Body which is made present substantially at the words of consecration. It is the Body of Christ with Whom we, being joined in Communion, form one mystical Person. The Eucharist, which prolongs the Incarnation among us, is the sign and cause of the Mystical Body which Christ has taken to Himself. Indeed, the most ancient commentary on the Mass, dating from the ninth century, tersely explains the words of the epiclesis: "That it may become to us the Body and Blood of Thy Beloved Son," by saying that these words point not only to the transubstantiation of the bread and wine, but also to our incorporation in Christ: they mean *"that we may become His Body* and that He may give us divinely in the mystery of divine grace, the Bread which descended from heaven."[3] The words recall St. Augustine's expression, in his exegesis of the 6th chapter of St. John: "The faithful know the Body of Christ if they do not neglect to become the body of Christ."[4]

The liturgy still tells us this truth in the Secret for the Mass of Corpus Christi:

"We beseech thee, O Lord, favorably grant Thy Church the gifts of unity and peace which are mystically designated beneath the gifts we offer."

Since this prayer is said at the end of the offertory, the reference is probably to the teaching of the Fathers, represented by St. Augustine, who says: "Our Lord fittingly gave us His Body and Blood under the species of things which are made one out of many. For the bread is one, though made of many grains; and the wine is one, though made of many grapes."[5] Hence the very natures

---

[3] 'Ut nobis corpus et sanguis fiat dilectissimi Filii': id est ut nos efficiamur corpus ejus, et nobis divinitus tradat in mysterio divinae gratiae panem qui de coelo descendit. Quoted by De Lubac, *Corpus Mysticum*, p. 33. cf. P.L. 138:1180.

[4] See above, page 96.

[5] *Tractatus 26, in Joannem*, P.L. 35: 1614, quoted by St. Thomas, *Summa Theologica* III, Q.69, a.1.

of bread and wine proclaim the purpose of the "sacramentum unitatis." However, it is clear that the mere fact that bread is made of many grains and the wine of many grapes does nothing of itself to effect our unity. It is only an aspect of the pedagogy of the Sacrament. What effects our mystical unity with one another is our sacramental eating of the true Body of Christ. Hence the sacramental sign of the unity of the mystical body is not to be sought in the species of bread or in the species of the wine. With regard to the unity of the Church, the sacramental species are only symbols in the ordinary sense, not *efficacious* signs. *The sign of our unity in Christ is the unity of Christ's own Body made present at every time and every place in which species are consecrated, and received in communion.* Hence, as modern theologians have pointed out, "Christ is a sign of Christ . . . Christ the one Man is the sign of Christ in whom the multitude of the elect are to be incorporated."[6]

St. John Chrysostom wrote a remarkable passage in which he brought out the intimate connection between the Eucharistic Body of Christ and the Mystical Body which is the Church. Speaking of the precious vessels of the altar and of the other liturgical objects by which we surround the Blessed

---

[6] From De La Taille's *Mystery of Faith*, Quoted by A-M Roguet, O.P., in La Maison Dieu, 24. "L'Unite dans la Charite-Res de l'Eucharistie," p. 27.

Sacrament with honor, the Greek Father pointed out that it was even more important to honor the body of Christ by giving alms to the poor. In this way, we are not only doing good to Him in the person of the poor, but we are making our own souls into sacred vessels of gold which give Him great glory. This was a thesis that was later to find an ardent defender in St. Bernard of Clairvaux. St. Chrysostom writes:

If you wish to honor the Eucharistic Victim, offer your own soul for which the Victim was immolated. Make your soul all of gold. If your soul remains viler than lead or clay, what good does it do to have a golden chalice...?

Do you wish to honor the Body of Christ? Then do not disdain Him when you see Him in rags. After having honored Him in Church with silken vestments do not leave Him to die of cold outside for lack of clothing. For it is the same Jesus Who says "This is my Body" and Who says "You saw me hungry and did not give me to eat—What you have refused to the least of these my little ones, you have refused it to me." The Body of Christ in the Eucharist demands pure souls, not costly garments. But in the poor He demands all our care. Let us act wisely; let us honor Christ as He Himself wishes to be honored: the most acceptable honor to one whom we would honor is the honor which He desires, not that which we ourselves imagine. Peter thought he was honoring his Master by not letting the Lord wash his feet; and yet it was just the opposite. Give Him then the honor which He Himself has asked for, by giving your money to the poor. Once again, what God wants is not golden chalices, but golden souls.[7]

The clearest summary of this teaching can be found in the *Summa Theologica* of St. Thomas. He tells us that the Eucharist is "the consummation of the spiritual life and the end of all the other sacraments"[8] since all the sacraments merely prepare us for the reception of the Eucharist, and this means that they lead us up to the sacred reality which the Eucharist alone can effect in us: perfect charity, consummate oneness in Christ. To say that all the sacraments culminate in the Eucharist is not to say, merely that they are rites which serve as preliminaries to the one great rite, the mystery of the cult. It means above all that the other sacraments give us *some part* in the charity of Christ, to fulfill certain particular needs of our own souls or of the souls of others, but that the Eucharist gives us the *fullness* of His charity, incorporates us perfectly in His Mystical Body, which lives by charity, and enables us thereby not only to receive charity directly from Christ our Mystical Head, but to rejoice in the life stream of charity which flows through the whole organism from one member to another.[9]

---

[7] St. John Chrysostom, Homily 50 on St. Matthew, 3.
[8] III, Q.73, a.2.
[9] III, Q.73, a.4.

Hence the Eucharist is in the strictest sense the *sacramentum pietatis,* the "sacrament of charity." For while in baptism man is regenerated by the Passion of Christ, in the Eucharist his charity is made perfect by sacramental participation in the charity of Christ. By the Eucharist "man is made perfect by union with Christ on the Cross"—*homo perficitur in unione ad Christum passum.*[10]

In Holy Communion, then, it is not we who transform the Body of Christ into ourselves, as happens with ordinary food: He on the contrary assimilates us and transforms us into Himself. But how? By incorporation, through charity, in His Mystical Body. While we "eat" the substance of the true Body of Christ under sacramental species, we ourselves are eaten and absorbed by the Mystical Body of Christ. We become as it were perfectly part of that Body, assimilated by it, one with its spiritual organism.[11]

This then is what St. Augustine meant when he exclaimed *O sacramentum pietatis*: "O sacrament of Love, O sign of Unity, O bond of charity! He who would have life finds here indeed a life to live *in* and a life to live *by*." And he adds "When men eat and drink, what they desire is not to hunger and not to thirst. But this effect is not really pro-

---

[10] III, Q.73, a.3 ad 3.
[11] *Ibid.,* ad 2.

duced except by the food and drink which render those who consume them immortal and incorruptible, and this food is the society of the saints where there will be peace and full and perfect unity.[12] The "sacred banquet" is then the banquet of charity, of fraternal unity in Christ. It is the sharing of Christ's love with one another: so that the strong help the weak to find Christ and the weak, in their turn, give the strong an opportunity to love Jesus more by loving Him in His members. Without these perspectives, our communions cannot attain the fullness and the joy that Christ desires them to have. As long as our love for Jesus in the Sacrament of His love is a love only for the Head, without sincere and warm affection for our brothers, without interest in the spiritual or physical needs of His members, our spiritual life will remain stunted and incomplete.

3. "I Have Called You My Friends"

No one who carefully reads the discourse at the Last Supper can help but be vividly impressed by

---

[12] Tractatus 26 in Joannem, P.L. 35:1613, 1614.

the special love of Jesus for the apostles He had chosen. He loves each one of them individually, He loves them as a group. They are "His own" whom He has loved "unto the end" (John 13:1). He washes their feet not only as an expression of His humility, but also and above all because if they are not "washed" with His own humble charity, they cannot have any part with Him (John 13:8). And then, sitting down at table, and preparing to break for the first time the Bread of the Eucharist which is His own Body, He tells them solemnly how important it is for them to love one another as He has loved them. This indeed is His great commandment, which sums up all the rest of His teaching and contains the full expression of His Father's will for us: that we should be *one in Him*. "By this shall all men know that you are My disciples, if you have love one for another" (John 13:35). "If you keep my commandments you shall abide in my love; as I also have kept my Father's commandments and abide in His love. . . . This is my commandment, that you love one another as I have loved you" (John 15:10–12).

Thus Jesus put the finishing touches on the formation of His apostles—a work that had become the major concern of the last year of His public life. The priest can find no purer and more complete manual of priestly spirituality than this discourse at the Last Supper, which contains all that

Christ Our Lord most fervently desired for the priests He ordained that night in the Cenacle. The whole program of the priestly life, as Jesus has exposed it here, is summed up in these two ideas: love Me as I have loved My Father—love one another as I have loved you. And the two can be reduced to one: *Abide in my love* (John 15:9).

It is quite true that this testament of charity was left by Jesus to His whole Church, but He left it in a more particular way to the priests whose whole life is one of eucharistic charity, union with Christ and with one another in Christ.

The life of every man is a mystery of solitude and communion: solitude in the secrecy of his own soul, where he is alone with God; communion with his brethren, who share the same nature, who reproduce in themselves his solitude, who are his "other selves" isolated from him and yet one with him. On the natural level, man's life is more of a solitude than a communion. Man fears solitude, yet the society in which he seeks refuge from his aloneness does not protect him adequately from his own insufficiency.

With the coming of Christ, man's solitude has become more perfect and more pure, in the sense that man has become more of a person; but he has become more of a person by virtue of his deeper union with other men in the charity of Christ.

In the heart of the priest, this mystery of solitude and communion reaches even greater depths.

No one was ever more terribly alone than Jesus among the men He had come to save. They could not understand Him, and as time went on they understood Him less and less. The Chosen People to whom He had been sent rejected Him—and they rejected Him through the priests and doctors of the Law who should have been the ones to recognize and receive Him. His apostles, who loved Him, nevertheless could not fathom His teaching and in the end ran away leaving Him to die alone.

Every priest shares to some extent in the solitude of the priestly heart of Jesus Christ. Isolated from other men by the priestly character and by the exalted level of his consecrated life, the priest is never allowed to forget that for him there is, strictly speaking, no profound and lasting consolation that is purely human and natural on this earth. He can enjoy friendships, indeed, but he well knows that unless these are spiritual and therefore in some sense marked with the sign of the Cross, they will serve only to accentuate his loneliness and embitter his poor heart.

At the same time, the priest enjoys a special spiritual authority over his people and humanly speaking he may be tempted to find in this a natural consolation for the loneliness of his heart. In that case, he likes to be "alone" in his exercise of authority. He wants to be the *only* father of the souls entrusted to him. He wants no one to forget that he, and he alone, is the shepherd. And so he may be tempted to desire for himself alone the consolations and rewards of his priestly ministry.

Christ has designed that the priestly life should be a eucharistic unity in all its aspects. It is never the individual minister who is really important, but Christ Himself, the One Priest, Who uses each priest as His instrument in His work for souls. Therefore Christ does not want His priests to be men of ambition, seeking glory and recognition for themselves and for their work, saying as the Pharisee said: "I am not like other men—I am not like other priests!"

And so, an essential aspect of the eucharistic life of the priest is his union, in priestly charity, with all those other Christs with whom he is one in the great High Priest.

Jesus formed the apostles as an intimate group who surrounded Him at all times during His public life. Not only was each one of them a beloved and trusted friend of the Lord, but also they were all meant to form a circle of friends, of brothers, loving one another because they were all loved by Him. This program was not perfectly realized. The Gospels tell us of several instances of jealousy and rivalry among them, which Jesus severely reproved. And this teaches us two things: that while priests will ever remain as human as the apostles themselves, and subject to the same human frailties, the will of Christ for them also remains the same. He keeps repeating to us the same lesson of humility and fraternal union. If we do not learn that lesson we cannot abide perfectly in His love. And if we do not abide in His love, the glory of the Father cannot be perfectly manifested in our lives (John 15:1–8).

We who have been chosen by Christ for the most exalted of all vocations must always keep in mind the fact that there is really only One Priest— Jesus Himself. Each one of us is only an instrument, a minister, of the Priesthood of Christ. Each one of us is, of course, another Christ: but all together we unite to form one "Christ," one anointed priest, and it is this "One Priest" Who truly gives glory to the Father by His homage of sacrifice and praise. We must take great care to purify our hearts of human and unconsciously pagan conceptions of the priesthood, as if it were something that could be acquired for ourselves by some particular virtue or power of our own. Our priesthood is not a power given to us for ourselves, as the result of a long esoteric training and initiation. It is rather the admission of each one of us into a mystical sharing of the priesthood of Christ. We are priests not for ourselves but for Him. Therefore we are priests also for one another. And therefore there should always be the most perfect harmony and unity among us. We should love one another, obey one another where the occasion permits or demands, humbly give in to one another, respect one another with a profound and sincere supernatural respect. We should try as far as possible to purify our hearts even of those unconscious and hidden jealousies, envies and resentments which may creep into our lives beneath the surface of cordiality and fraternal good will with which we maintain the appearance of friendly co-operation.

All this demands great sacrifices of us, sacrifices more difficult than many which we willingly assume in our work for the salvation of souls. But it will also bring with it great and supernatural consolations. It will bring strength in Christ, a new sense of the unity and purpose of our vocation, a realization of the power of Christ living and acting in His Church.

For these reasons our meditations before the Blessed Sacrament, our moments of recollection after Mass, our recitation of the Office and above all our daily Mass should be penetrated with this spirit of priestly charity, this sense of unity with our brother-priests everywhere, of true submission to our superiors, and of total abandonment of ourselves to the will of Christ, our High Priest.

This means the greatest constancy in self-renunciation, a thing which is not possible without a deep, even an heroic faith in the eucharistic Christ.

4. The New Commandment

If we love the Blessed Sacrament, and if we delight to spend our time in adoration of this tremendous mystery of love, we cannot help finding out more and more about the charity of Christ. We cannot help gaining an intimate and personal knowledge of Jesus Who is hidden under the sacramental veils. But in proportion as we grow in our knowledge and love for Him, we will necessarily grow in the knowledge of His will for us. We will come to understand more and more how seriously He means us to take His "new commandment" that we love one another as He has loved us.

Indeed, if we fail to take this commandment seriously and if we find our devotional life concentrated upon a selfish desire for pious feelings that enclose us within ourselves and narrow our heart, making us insensible to others or even contemptuous of them, we can be sure that our devotion is an illusion. We do not know Christ because we do not keep His word. For he only manifests Himself to those who do His will. And He wills to come to us in this Sacrament of His love not only in order to console us as individuals, but in order that we may give Him our hearts and let Him dwell in them, that through us He may love our brothers with our own love.

Since the will of the Father, the entire salvific plan of God, terminates in the resurrection and glorification of the whole Mystical Body, it is clear that the Blessed Eucharist is given to us first of all that we may become perfect in charity ourselves, and then that our charity may communicate itself as a life-giving spiritual energy to other souls throughout the whole Church. Nor does Christ wait until we become perfect in love, before He makes our love bear fruit in the lives of others. It is by loving others that we grow in love for Him, and by loving Him, especially by entering deeply into the Mystery of the Cross and of the Eucharist, that we grow in our capacity to love others.

Hence the sacred banquet of the Eucharist is the expression not only of the spiritual growth and joy of individuals, but of the vitality of the whole Church. It is around the table at which Christ again breaks bread for His disciples that the children of the Church grow in age and grace before God and men, and attain to the full stature of the maturity of Christ.

Commenting on some of the great texts of St. Paul on the unity of the Mystical Body (for instance, I Corinthians 10:17 and Ephesians 4:15–16), St. Thomas distinguishes between different aspects of our oneness in Christ. We are one with Him by faith, which incorporates us in Him, by hope and charity which make us grow in Him. Over and above this we are one with Him in a unity of life and thought *(vitae et sensus)* which is manifested by works of charity with which we aid one another, and by agreement on the truths of faith and morals. Finally, the most intimate union between us is sealed by the particular action of each one, according to his vocation in Christ.

Each one of us is called to play a special part (even though that part may seem hidden and unimportant) in the building up of the body of Christ. The supernatural actions by which we carry on the work entrusted to us bind us more and more closely with the other members of the body in fraternal cooperation. And these deeds proceed from the hidden movement of Christ within our souls—the action of special graces, graces of state, graces proper to our own peculiar and individual vocation within the Church.

It is to be noticed that the movement of these special graces by which we fulfill our duties of state and carry on our work for Christ, are orientated away from our own private and particular good, and towards the good of all—that is to say towards charity and towards God. Yet at the same time it is precisely these movements of grace which enable us to fulfill our own personal destiny most perfectly. We truly become our real selves by living for others in Christ. In living for Christ and His Church we are at the same time living for others and for ourselves. The highest good of all is Christ Himself, living in us one and all, and acting on us all to produce a common charity in all our hearts by the movements of the Spirit which knit us more and more perfectly together in Christ. This charity flows into our souls above all from the Holy Eucharist. It is the effect of our sacramental contacts with the sacred Body of Christ, the fruit of our union with His most holy soul and with the divinity of the Logos in this greatest of all sacraments.

St. Bonaventure says:

Just as God takes care of the bodies of all living things, providing them with suitable foods, so too He takes care of the most noble Body of His Son, which is the Church, and Whose Head is Christ the Son of God. That Body cannot live and be nourished from any other source than from this Head, so that all the members, that is all just men, united and integrated together in Christ the Head, should be nourished by His Spirit and by His love through this Sacrament of unity and peace. And thus, just as no body can live without taking into itself food which agrees with it, so too there is no life for the rational soul except by eating and taking to itself this spiritual food which is what it needs. Hence Christ says: He who eats me shall live by me.[13]

In short Christ comes to us in this sacrament to finish the work His Father gave Him to do. He comes to us to fill our souls with that charity which led Him to die for us on the Cross. He comes to live in our hearts and to lead us to the one end to which all rightly ordered human activity tends: the love of God and the love of our neighbor in God. If we will respond to His love, if we will let this divine Sacrament purify our hearts of all attachment to worldly things, He will make us stronger and more resolute in loving Him. He will teach us to understand not only His love for us, but His love for our neighbor. He will teach us to see into the depths of our brother's heart, by humility and self-effacing compassion. He will teach us that it is not enough to bear with the frailties and the sins of others, we must also love them even unto the death of the Cross. As Christ came to die for us when we were all His enemies, we no longer have any excuse for willfully hating any man. As Christ came to overcome evil with good, so we too, nourished by this Sacrament, will learn that the charity of Christ is strong enough to reach out and embrace

---

[13] *De Praeparatione ad Missam,* i, 13.

even our enemies and His, strong enough to conquer them and turn them from enemies into friends.

5. Toward the Parousia

As long as we are in this world, our life in Christ
remains hidden. Our union in Him also remains
hidden. Hidden too is Christ's reality in the Eucharist, and in His Church. His presence, often denied
and derided by mere reason, is evident only to faith.
But our meditations on the Blessed Sacrament
would remain incomplete if we did not remind ourselves that this is only a transient condition. He
Who is hidden has said that He will manifest Himself. Our knowledge of Christ by faith, our hidden
union with Him, these are not the end of the journey but only its beginning. We look for the coming
of Christ. We are the ones who, as St. Paul says,
"love His advent" (II Timothy 4:8). That means
to say that we who possess Him by faith, and are
united with Him by faith, are always looking forward to the day when what is hidden presence will
be revealed plainly, and what is secret will become
manifest. In a word, we live in the hope of a glori-

ous manifestation of the great mystery of Christ. We hope for the "appearance" of the whole Christ —the *Parousia*.

Jesus solemnly declared, when He was on trial before the Sanhedrin, that the Son of Man would be seen one day "sitting at the right hand of the Power and coming upon the clouds of heaven" (Matthew 26:64). The mysterious figurative language in which the Synoptic Gospels speak of the Second Coming of Christ and of the Last Judgment is clarified to some extent by the theological elaboration which it receives from St. Paul. In the mind of the Apostle of the Gentiles, the Parousia and Last Judgment will be the clear manifestation of Christ in His Body the Church. In other words, the Last Judgment will be the final consummation and revelation of the "Mystery"—the re-establishment of all things in Christ, that is being accomplished in secret beneath the surface of human history.

There is a certain false mysticism which likes to gloat over the prospect of a Last Judgment in which the whole history of mankind will fall into oblivion under the anathema of an enraged God. But the true Christian viewpoint is that which looks forward to the Last Judgment as the clarification and vindication of human history. The Parousia is the great event which will not destroy human history but fulfill it, explaining everything that was not clear, showing how all things worked together for the good of Christ and fulfilled the purposes of the Father. Then we will see how wise were the Providential decrees of God permitting what seemed to be incomprehensible evils. We will see that the judgments of God were wiser and more merciful than the judgments of man, and that His wisdom was deeper than the wisdom of the wise and powerful. All truth will be vindicated, all real values will be recognized and shown for what they were, no matter where they may have existed.

Christ has told us not to expect His Parousia to be the glorification of all the respectable citizens who received salutations in the market place and the first places at banquets. Indeed, many will come from the east and the west and sit down at the banquet of heaven, while those who were only exteriorly respectable will hear Christ say to them: "the publicans and harlots are entering into the kingdom of heaven before you" (Matthew 21:31).

The Parousia will be at once the judgment of the good and the evil and the manifestation of the whole Christ. Those who were truly good will be found in the light of Christ, and those who were truly evil will be found in the darkness without Christ, no matter what may have been their respective reputations among men. And the difference between them will be, above all, the difference in the quality of their love. Did they love God and did they love other men? Did they truly seek the true Good? Did they seek it in God? Then they will be found "in Christ" and He will be revealed in them.

The Parousia will indeed be the manifestation of Christ in us and of us in Christ. It will fulfill the words of the Spirit speaking through St. Paul: "When Christ your life shall appear, then you too will appear with Him in glory" (Colossians 3:4).

We said at the beginning of this book that the Eucharist is a sign of this final consummation. That is only another way of saying that at the Parousia the *res sacramenti* of the Eucharist, will be made fully manifest. The Mystical Body of Christ, of which His Sacramental Body is the "sign," will be seen for what it is. The hidden interconnection between the two mysteries will finally resolve itself into the light of vision in which we will see how the two "Bodies of Christ" are in fact one: how the Sacramental Christ is the living heart of His Mystical Body, and how all who have been united by partaking in the substance of His Body are in fact One Body in Him. This will be the beginning of that sacred banquet in which our joy will no longer be hidden in the darkness of faith and muted by the silences of hope, but will break forth into the everlasting song of glory and of victory which is the *Alleluia* of the Church triumphant.

Meanwhile, even while we are in the midst of the battle, we must realize that the very presence of the Eucharist in the world has turned man's history, at least the history of the elect, into a *sacrum convivium*. There is no reason to despair of man or of human society. The fact that the mystery of iniquity is at work in the world is no reason for the Christian to take the attitude that human society, as such, is irrevocably doomed and that the time has come for the gentiles to be crushed and trampled in the wine press of fierce retribution.

No true Christian can safely face the Last Judgment with the self-satisfied conviction that it is "somebody else" who is wicked, and that certain "other people" are foredoomed to be among the goats. If we are members of Christ, then we must live as members of Christ. We must be like Him Who came not to condemn man in his misery and confusion, but to enlighten him and save him.

Our life in Christ, therefore, calls for a fully eucharistic apostolate—a far-seeing and energetic action, based on prayer and interior union with God, which is able to transcend the limitations of class, and nation, and culture and continue to build a new world upon the ruins of what is always falling into decay.

If the future seems dark to us, is it not perhaps because we are witnessing the dawn of a light that has never before been seen? We live in an age in which charity can become heroic as it has never been before. We live, perhaps, on the threshold of the greatest eucharistic era of the world—the era that may well witness the final union of all mankind.

If that is true, then we are within the reach of a tremendous fulfillment: the visible union close to the whole world in Christ. This fulfillment, far from being foreign to eucharistic spirituality, is of its very essence. Mass and communion do not make sense unless we remember that the Eucharist is the great means which God has devised for gathering together and unifying mankind, dispersed by original and actual sin. The Eucharist is the sacrament of unity, and the eucharistic life by its very nature, is orientated towards an apostolate of charity which will effect a visible union of all mankind. Will this visible union be a political one? Is that a possibility to be hoped for, or is it one of the temptations of the world's final age? These are questions I am not prepared to answer, and the end of a book is perhaps not the proper place for me to raise them. Christ's Kingdom is "not of this world" and it is certainly true that many who pretend to be working for a politically united mankind are also relentless enemies of the Eucharist, the priesthood and the Church. Perhaps the last age of all will be "eucharistic" in the sense that the Church herself will give the glory and praise to God by being put to the Cross. But in that case, she will only do as the Redeemer did before her, and open her arms to all mankind and bring them to unity and victory in her own apparent defeat.

The man who can truly say he looks forward with hope and joy to the Parousia of the Son of God is the man whose eucharistic life bears fruit in prayer and labor for the union of all mankind in Christ. In working to unite all men in charity, we are as it were preparing the Host, made up of many grains, to be finally consecrated and transformed in the glory of Christ at the end of time. It was for this that Jesus Himself prayed to the Father at the Last Supper (John 17:20-23):

Not for these only do I pray, but for those also who through their word are to believe in me, that all may be one, even as thou, Father, in me and I in thee; that they also may be one in us, that the world may believe that thou hast sent me. And the glory that thou hast given me, I have given to them, that they may be one, even as we are one: I in them and thou in me; that they may be perfected in unity, and that the world may know that thou hast sent me, and that thou hast loved them even as thou hast loved me.